Sue,
Thank you!
for everything!.
This work would not is
possible without my time with
you. I am ME because
you believed in me!
I Love you,
Christy

Oh God of Second Chances
Chances
Here I Am Again

ADVANCED PRAISE FOR OH GOD OF SECOND CHANCES

"Oh God of Second Chances is brilliant and something we all need....the invitation to know the grace we've been given, the chance to connect to our courage and the tenacity to begin again."

- Aspen DeCew, *A Voice to the Voices* at *"Truly Conscious"*

"A masterclass in courage, if you've ever wondered how to live well, this is the book you've been waiting for. With heartfelt wisdom and an infectious, humble sense of humor, Christy Belz made me feel like I was sitting down with my best friend to take honest, yet gentle, stock of my life. Pulling inspiration from wide-ranging sources--TEDx speakers, her own wild (and I mean WILD!) life, and The Wizard of Oz alike--this book is more than an invitation to second chances. It's an invitation to endless chances, and to full-throttle, don't-hold-back living. A real trove of riches."

- Laura Thomas, author of *The Magic of Well-Being*

"Where would we be without sisterhood? While I was not blessed to have biological sisters, I am blessed to have a village of sisters-by-choice. In this book, I hear the stories of many women who are lifted up by other women or who lift others up with their stories of inspiration. Women empowerment is key. We are better together."

- Dr. Sally Spencer-Thomas, Author, Professional Speaker on Workplace Mental Health, Podcaster & Impact Entrepreneur

ADVANCED PRAISE FOR OH GOD OF SECOND CHANCES

"I loved this book the first time I read it! I loved it the second, third and fourth time even more! Christy packed this book full of riveting stories of how she and others faced life's challenges and how they worked them out, healed, and prevailed. It's absolutely loaded with clear, doable advice, helpful resources and awakening wisdom. I learn something each time I open it. It just keeps on giving...."

- Phyllis Mitz, M.A. Astrologer and Author of *Love Stars: Astrology's Secrets to Relationships, Compatibility and* **Great Sex!**

"Christy is such a bright light whose voice of love and heartfelt connection shines through. She is a guide who constantly reminds you to learn and grow with the community of support around you, most of all, she teaches you to align with yourself! This is a must-read."

- Phoenix Jackson, CEO at and author of, *The Phoenix Affect*

"Get ready to experience the ups and downs of your emotions, from laughter to tears, as Christy takes you with her in this heart opening book. She shares her journey in Earth School to enlighten all of us with her insights as well as wisdom from the many teachers who inspired her. Her curiosity and vulnerability are inspiring!"

- Cathy Hawk, Award winning Author, Founder Clarity International, Executive Coach, Teacher.

ADVANCED PRAISE FOR OH GOD OF SECOND CHANCES

"To know Christy Belz is to know one of today's top modern day spiritual teachers. I put her in the same company as Eckhart Tole and Don Miquel Ruiz. Her book "Oh God of Second Chances Here I am Again" is an easy read that celebrates one's imperfections and presents opportunities to create something even more beautiful with your life."

- Jen Lester, Co-founder, Philosophy Communication

"Christy has shared a brilliant gift with us – an enhanced ability to lead with our heart. She offers practical techniques and compelling stories, and most of all, Christy shares her heart with us. Her courage to find the beauty in being raw and the strength to find her voice is inspiring. This book is for everyone regardless of where you are on your journey of living the best version of yourself."

- Gretchen Gagel, PhD, President Greatness Consulting

"I am who I am today in large part due to Christy Belz. Christy is my "go-to" for healing and helping with challenges. She listens to me, her intuition, and higher guidance always offering wisdom that helps me to move to a healthier place. As I read "Oh God of Second Chances!" I smiled because some of the stories, words, and solutions are familiar, and have already helped me immensely! (This Stuff Works!) I also smiled as I discovered new to me nuggets, information, and processes to serve me in the future. This book is "so Christy," written authentically, vulnerably, and courageously. I could hear her voice in my head as I read the words! Thank you, Christy!"

- Pat Jacques, ADV women

ADVANCED PRAISE FOR OH GOD OF SECOND CHANCES

"Christy's book took me on a healing journey through the power of her own story. Beautifully woven with research from other thought leaders and her own, this power-filled book not only gave me validation of the importance of my own imperfection, put showed me the possibility that I can live into my greatest self. It is tender, raw, funny and a gathering of life truths you do not want to miss!"

- Betsy Wiersma, Philanthropist, Author, Speaker and Artist

"By vulnerably sharing stories of brokenness and second chances in her own life, Christy gave me permission to embrace my own stories and find a way forward to wholeness and life-giving purpose. She wants this for us all!"

- Karen Bensen, Associate Professor of the Practice of Social Work at University of Denver Graduate School of Social Work

"This book combines the vulnerability, strength, and storytelling of a woman who has not only heard and seen it all, but experienced it all too. Fantastic stories with brilliant lessons for us all to learn from"

- Haley Skiko, TEDx Speaker

"Working with the amazing group with TEDx Women Cherry Creek inspired me to be the most courageous version of myself in sharing my story. Christy (Belz) is a mentor to me, and her writing captures the essence of my passion in destigmatizing behavioral health issues. This is a must-read for all.

- Dr Nikki Dority

Oh God of Second Chances Chances Here I Am Again

CHRISTY BELZ

Guide Point North Publishing
An Imprint of Journey Institute Press

Guide Point North Publishing
An imprint of Journey Institute Press, a division of
50 in 52 Journey, Inc.

journeyinstitutepress.com

Library of Congress Control Number: 2022937009

Names: Belz, Christy
Title: Oh God of Second Chances, Here I Am Again
Description: Colorado: Guide Point North Publishing, 2022
Identifiers: ISBN 978-1-7373591-8-0 (hardcover)
Subjects: BISAC: SOCIAL SCIENCE / Women's Studies |
PSYCHOLOGY / Social Psychology |
SELF-HELP / Personal Growth / Happiness.

First Edition
Printed in the United States of America

Typeset: Adobe Caslon Pro, Brandon Grotesque

Book Cover http://www.judymackey.com/

Dear friends, of which I am so blessed with many, you are my greatest fans! Thank you.

This book would not have been possible without the TEDx-CherryCreek team. Dafna and Michael, what a journey and wonderful adventure to steward the TEDxCherryCreek speakers on the extraordinary adventure of speaking on the TEDx stage. Your talents have been the best, bar none, in the curation and production of these events. To the team of TEDx, from our event staff to our volunteers and, most importantly, our speakers, you all have inspired me in so many ways. From service to sacrifice behind the scenes, to courageous authenticity on the stage—it was nothing short of amazing.

This book certainly would not have been written without the talents of Jessie Lucier, who outlined the book from my TEDx Talk and helped write the first few chapters. Laura Thomas, also a contributor with her TEDx Talk feature, brought it home with her gifts and talents to complete the work. Thank you to both of you!

Finally, my husband. You have been the glue and the rock and the brick I needed not only to share my life, our life, with the world, but you are the greatest blessing in my life. Your steadfast way, your sturdiness and your amazing love for me on this journey of love and life has made all the difference. Having you and Charlie in my life brings me all that I ever desired . . . A family, a love, and a home. I love you.

CONTENTS

Introduction: The Power of New Beginnings

Drench yourself in words unspoken
Live your life with arms wide open
Today is where your book begins
The rest is still unwritten
—Natasha Bedingfield, *"Unwritten"*

Before you begin reading, I invite you to give yourself permission to pause. Take a deep breath and connect to your breathing. Connect with your body and start to allow yourself to relax. Come into this very moment, be here now.

This simple practice—this is where it all begins. In this space, we can begin. We can begin again and again.

I call this exercise Permission to Pause. It is the simplest way to bring myself into the present moment, to feel ME, "My Essence," and to connect with the Source of my being. There was a time when it felt impossible for me to relax without judgment and just be with myself. I tried for years to sit still, clear my head, and trust that I was being led to nirvana. Time after time, in workshops, retreats, and in my own meditation space at home, I waited and waited for that inner peace to come . . .

One day, in my home office between clients, I sat quietly with my eyes closed and tried to go into a meditative space. Finally, I realized what was happening—I was meditating! I had practiced meditation hundreds of times, yet had never really *felt it*. Now, do you know what I felt? *Nothing!* The "no-thing" that I had been reaching for all this time. And do you know what else? I felt pissed! Even though I was experiencing what I had been taught to expect—a kind of quietness and stillness—I had been hoping for some sort of choir-singing-Hallelujah mystical experience. But the actuality of meditation and mindfulness was not flashy; it was really . . . simple.

Now, decades later, I understand and appreciate the value of being able to get still.

Saying we want to get still and connect with our breath, bodies, and hearts and actually doing it can be two hugely different things, especially for women. Many of the women in my life—whether they are the women I see as clients, those I work with professionally, or my dear friends—are often what I refer to as "stressed, depressed, and unexpressed." They hold themselves back from fully living and thriving. I know that I have certainly been there . . .

As women living in an increasingly crazy external world, we often struggle. We struggle with shame, blame, and guilt. We struggle with insecurities or thinking we are "too much" or "too little." We struggle with unresolved trauma, anxiety, depression, body image issues and eating disorders, relationships, and addictions. And many—if not most—of us struggle to cultivate the deep self-compassion we need to make sense of and grow from all the experiences in our lives. Life can feel cruel, scary, ugly, and deeply confusing at times, but it can also be a beautiful experience of growth and joy—if we let it. A big part of the equation is allowing ourselves to fall down, engage in a radical process of self-forgiveness and self-compassion, and then get the hell up and try again!

I titled this book *Oh God of Second Chances: Here I Am Again,* but, in all honesty, it should be called *Oh God of 25,000 Chances: Here I Am for The Gazillionth Time.* I cannot tell you how many times I have fallen down—mentally, emotionally, spiritually, and physically—and thanked God, the Divine, the goddesses, the angels, the Universe—whatever or whomever you prefer to call Spirit—for the power of new beginnings. In every moment and with every breath, we have the power and the awesome ability to begin again. I know it doesn't seem that way when we feel alone, like we are the only one making colossal mistakes. It appears everyone else has it all together and that we are doomed to keep falling down without any sort of reprieve.

So many of us feel isolated in our mistakes and shameful stories, thinking that it is "just me." I am the only one who fights with my husband or has a child who can be dismissive and aloof. I am the only one who struggles with the aging process and the donut that has taken over my waistline. I am the only one who feels like I am not good enough, or just not enough at all.

I am the only one who has unresolved trauma and a challenging family of origin. I am the only one who has made all these stupid mistakes. Surely, no one else has had a one-night stand, or stayed too long in the wrong relationship, or chose the wrong person to date in the first place. Who else has gotten so drunk that they threw up and could not get out of bed the next day? Or snorted so much coke that they had a panic attack? Or did not show up to see their grandmothers over the holidays because they had not slept in two days?

Who else has felt alone and ashamed because of their mistakes?

I felt alone for a long time. Now, after years of working with, connecting with, and developing close relationships with women, I know that I was not really alone, no matter what I was going through. We all have our insecurities, inner critics, and past behaviors that we are not proud of. We have all made mistakes and have done and said things we wish we could take back. We have all prayed for a redo. But, in many ways, it is through our mistakes that we develop a willingness to get back up, reassemble the broken pieces, and create something stronger and even more beautiful than before.

For the better part of my life, I did not share many of my stories because I was not proud of them, nor did I find them funny. It is different today, though. After decades of working as a social worker and women's leadership and empowerment coach, I know we all have stories that we are not proud of. Yet, we all carry around this crazy belief that "it is just me." In our self-shaming voices, we think that we are the only one with problems, and there must be something terribly wrong with us. This inner critic causes us to internalize our shame. Shame—that self-defeating bedrock below all other emotions—keeps us in the past, feeling that there must be something innately wrong with us. Shame makes us even more fearful of an uncertain future and denies us the capacity and compassion to claim our authentic selves.

So, what can we do about it? How can we sift and shift through this cultural phenomenon of the "just me" mentality that keeps too many of us playing small and stuck in our heads?

For starters, we can talk about it. We can give ourselves permission to truly be seen. We can talk with other women. We can start conversations about what it is like to be a woman in today's crazy world. We can do what scares us and put our stories out into the world for other women to read. We can connect with each other. We can support each other. We can celebrate each other. And we can serve.

We can also stop minimizing our experiences while also owning our mistakes. We can celebrate ourselves and each other when we fall down and get up again for the second or 25,000th time. And we can find humor in it all. It is humor that truly makes me love the title of this book. I still laugh every time I glance at it. *Oh God of Second Chances: Here I Am Again.* Oh God, it is so true. There is grace in all the opportunities we have to get up and do this life again, albeit a little more worn, but wiser every time. Even after having so many shit mornings lying in bed agonizing over drinking too much, or saying something that I wish I did not, or feeling like I was failing as a partner, parent, or friend, today I relish in the wisdom that I get to choose again. Spirit never tires of giving us second chances.

I must admit that today, on the outside, my life looks pretty good. I have a wonderful, successful husband and a beautiful son. I have achieved personal and professional success. I have amazing, loyal friends and belong to a progressive and vibrant community. I am well-resourced enough to be considered privileged by most. And I truly know how blessed I am. I can see how, on the outside, it appears that I have it all together (which, by the way, is not always the most enjoyable way to be perceived). Yet, the truth is that I do not. I am sometimes still that ten-year-old girl who saw her father being carted away by EMTs after trying to take his own life. I am still that wild young woman drinking Budweiser, smoking Marlboro Lights, and chasing after the bad boys in their tight jeans and cowboy boots. I am still that sales professional turned social worker, following her heart while pursuing passion over stability.

Traveling the Twists and Turns of the Yellow Brick Road

This book is about falling down and having the courage to get up and do it again. It is my sincere hope that, by reading these pages, you will realize that you are not alone—have never been alone—and that there is an abundance of second chances. You are and have always been guided, supported, and loved. You are whole, perfect, and complete, all of the time, no matter what. You are a child of the Universe, and you never walk alone.

It takes great courage, vulnerability, and heart to share our stories, and, for many women, these stories include tales of trauma; abuse; illness; social, gender, and racial inequity; eating disorders; addictions; loss; grief; and death. Yet, the stories of our lives also include overcoming and rising above incredible challenges so we can heal, begin new initiatives, become leaders in our communities, and take action to inspire women of all walks. Our stories can heal and inspire, encourage and soothe. That is why I have included additional voices in this book. Near the end of each chapter, you will find a featured TEDx Talk from another woman. These are women I have been privileged enough to coach on the TEDx stage whose stories have literally changed my life. They are raw and honest, and I know they will have something meaningful to offer you as you walk your journey to a full, authentic self.

The title of this book truly is my daily mantra. *Oh God of Second Chances, Here I Am Again.* These words help me recognize, day in and day out, that we all, as imperfect beings, are also divinely created. As Spirit walks with us, even when we fall down, screw up, or let personal or global negativity permeate our psyches, we are also given grace—a hand that says, "It is okay, get up, let's try again."

I wish I could say that the process of personal, professional, and spiritual growth is easy. It is not. Leading from the heart is not for the faint of heart. Walking the path to your authentic self takes courage. As a Kansas native, I am a big fan of *The Wizard of Oz*, and you will find themes from that great story throughout the book. My favorite character is the Cowardly Lion, always on the quest for courage. I have a sign in my office with butterfly wings, and in the middle, it reads "Hello Courage." It reminds me every day that feeling discomfort, leaning into my vulnerabilities, and opening and sharing my soul through stories takes great courage. I hope that by sharing my stories, you will feel your fear and do it anyway. For, as Glinda the Good Witch says, "You've always had the power, my dear, you just had to learn it for yourself."[1]

Along the twists, turns, stumbles, and successes of my personal yellow brick road, I have cultivated a wonderful array of tools and techniques that have helped transform my life and the lives of those with whom I have worked. Throughout the book, you will find practices designed to help you give yourself permission to pause, connect with your heart, step more fully into yourself, practice insane courage, and live more fully as your authentic, absolutely powerful, and beautiful self.

Here is to three clicks of your ruby red cowboy boots as you find your way back home . . .

With love and in solidarity,
Christy

1

A Little Courage, Please

"You have plenty of courage, I am sure," answered Oz. "All you need is confidence in yourself. There is no living thing that is not afraid when it faces danger. The true courage is in facing danger when you are afraid, and that kind of courage you have in plenty."
—L. Frank Baum, *The Wonderful Wizard of Oz*

This book began with courage. The courage to write it. The courage to tell my story. The courage to write boldly and bravely about being scared. Scared of uncertainty. Scared to be vulnerable. Scared of violence. I have been afraid of the unknown, of being judged, of being made a fool. I have feared that I did not and could not fit in, was not smart enough, good enough, or pretty enough. And although I still feel scared at times, I know now that living from a place of fear has not, does not, and will not serve me. All it does is keep me believing I am not safe and feeling small.

Born and raised in Kansas, I am a big fan of rodeos, cowboy boots, men in tight blue jeans, BBQ, and, of course, *The Wizard of Oz*. My favorite character—as I mentioned—is the Cowardly Lion. I call on his archetype often. I love the Lion's character, particularly because I know it takes great courage to live a fulfilling and meaningful life.

But what is courage, really?

Courage is defined as the ability to do something that you know is difficult or dangerous. More specifically, Merriam-Webster defines courage as "mental or moral strength to venture, persevere, and withstand danger, fear, or difficulty."[1] I think that demonstrating courage requires the mental and moral strength to live with truth in a complicated and complex world, but ultimately, courage comes through the heart. To tap into, listen to, and follow our hearts rather than our heads is the most courageous thing we can do.

Like the Cowardly Lion learns, we cannot get to where we are meant to go—where our hearts want to lead us—without courage. Living a full life requires that we fully experience our feelings, get uncomfortable, show our true selves, and take empowered actions toward our dreams, goals, and purpose. Being courageous is not easy. Living on this planet is hard. It is tough trying to navigate all the systems and structures. Dang, it takes courage some days just to get out of bed.

But to live fully, grow, move forward, and develop our potential, we must feel more deeply, expand our resilience and tolerance, and bravely step into our lives. If we want deeper relationships with others and with ourselves and an enhanced ability to connect with our hearts, we must tap into our truest desires, connect with the wisdom of the heart, and employ courage.

It is my belief that our futures are predicated on our desires, which come from our hearts and an innate sense of knowing. In Luke 12:32, the Bible says, "It is your Father's good pleasure to give you the Kingdom."[2] In Matthew 7:7, the Bible also says, "Ask, and it shall be given to you."[3]

What is it that *you* desire?

What does *your* heart long for?

What scares you and would require courage and faith to pursue?

Our hearts are all-knowing. Yet, we tend to trust in our cognitive thinking—the product of our nonstop, dynamic, worry-ridden brains—rather than the innate wisdom of the heart, which is where true courage resides. We are rarely taught to lead from the heart. Doing so goes against the status quo of the "intelligent" systems, structures, and constructs that comprise our cultural "truths." We are taught to abide by these socialized systems, drawing from external sources to make decisions based on what we have been taught is right rather than what we inherently know to be true.

In *A Whole New Mind: Why Right-Brainers Will Rule the Future*, author Daniel H. Pink writes, "The future belongs to a very different kind of person with a very different kind of mind—creators and empathizers, pattern recognizers, and meaning makers." He continues, "We are moving from an economy and a society built on the logical, linear, computerlike capabilities of the Information Age to an economy and a society built on the inventive, empathic, big-picture capabilities of what is rising in its place, the Conceptual Age."[4]

If, as Pink writes, we are truly in the midst of shifting from fact-based, data-driven, "computer like" ways of being to an increased focus on right-brain function, we need courage. It takes courage to change. As Pink says, "Change is inevitable, and when it happens, the wisest response is not to wail or whine but to suck it up and deal with it."

In her 2007 book, *I Thought It Was Just Me (But It Isn't): Making the Journey from "What Will People Think?" to "I Am Enough,"* researcher, storyteller, and bestselling author Brené Brown explains courage this way:

> Courage is a heart word. The root of the word courage is *cor*—the Latin word for heart. In one of its earliest forms, the word courage meant "To speak one's mind by telling all one's heart." Over time, this definition has changed, and today we typically associate courage with heroic and brave deeds. But this definition fails to recognize the inner strength and level of commitment required for us to speak honestly and openly about who we are and about our experiences—good and bad. Speaking from our hearts is what I think of as "ordinary courage."[5]

As Brown shares, courage is a heart word. I love this. I have always been a big believer in the heart—that it is powerful and all-knowing if we allow it to be. The heart knows the answer to everything. It is the focal point of the authentic self. When we trust our hearts and lead with courage, we are guided in the direction of living as our most loving and authentic selves.

Just so you know, you are going to be hearing a lot about Brené Brown in this book. She has been tremendously influential in my life and work. When I was in graduate school for social work—six months pregnant with my son—I felt out of place. I kept wondering why I was not pursuing an MBA instead. After all, I had a successful business background. I love the values of social work and the focus on the whole person rather than just on their psychoses. However,

I was frustrated with how the field was devalued, both by society as a whole and within the not-for-profit sector.

When Brown came on the scene in 2010 with her popular TEDx Talk about vulnerability, there was a meaningful change in the social work field. Suddenly, more people recognized that social workers could be thought leaders, too. Brown is not the only amazing social worker who has taken on this role. One of my mentors, Dr. Jean F. East, co-led a not-for-profit agency where I was privileged to work after completing graduate school.

Dr. East published several research articles, and most recently, she wrote a textbook titled *Transformational Leadership for the Helping Professions—Engaging Head, Heart, and Soul.* I had the honor of sharing my professional journey in a chapter. She also did a TEDx Talk on this work called "Leading with Head, Heart, and Soul."

Brown certainly leads with her head, heart, and soul. The depth of her research on shame and vulnerability brought validity to the field of social work. I loved what she was doing so much that I have now seen her five times in person. I've read and reread all her books, and I am trained in her work. I often contextualize my ideas through her thought leadership and research. Plus, I admire her as a person. She pushes herself to live with great authenticity and courage.

Living With Courage

It can be tough trying to navigate this thing called life. Most of us struggle with stress, fear, and uncertainty, trying to control things that we really have no power over. With so many moving parts—our relationships, marriages, careers, children, finances, goals, and dreams—life can feel overwhelming and scary at times. As women, we also tend to struggle with boundaries. We might be empaths and attract people who suck our energy. Or we are over-givers, feeling underappreciated, undervalued, and exhausted. Sometimes we do not really know what we want. It is hard for us to make decisions or stick to the decisions that we do make. We are often riddled with doubt, not knowing whether to turn right or left. Does that sound familiar?

It took a lot of heart and courage for me to leave a well-paying, successful job in advertising to pursue my passion for helping people. Finally, after agonizing over the decision, I used the courage of the Cowardly Lion, quit my job, and started college using money from my 401(k). People thought I was crazy! Many of my friends and family members could not understand why I was leaving all that I had worked so hard to achieve at an early age, all to pursue a degree in social work.

I did not go to college right out of high school. College was not planned for me or discussed in my family. My mother did not graduate from high school, and my dad went right into military service. My brother, Mike, dropped out of high school as well. When I was hired at an advertising agency, I started at entry level. I grew with the company until I was promoted to several new positions, ultimately ending up in sales.

During my frequent trips to the East Coast for work, I was often asked two questions when meeting someone new. The first was where I was from. "Kansas," I would proudly answer. "And no, I do not have cows in my backyard." The second question was where I went to college. I hated that question. It created a great deal of shame for me. Not having gone to college—and not even recognizing at an early age that it was even possible—really bothered me and flooded my mind with questions. Why hadn't I gone to college? Why was not college considered or even talked about as a possibility for me? Was there something inherently wrong with me? Was I not smart enough?

These questions lingered even as I pursued an incredible career. Despite my success in the eyes of society, friends, family, and colleagues, I was not happy. I was exhausted and feeling stressed, depressed, and underexpressed. On the exterior, I was doing well in every way, but on the inside, I had no idea who I was or what my true purpose was in this life. I did, however, know that there had to be something more.

During that confusing period of young womanhood, I discovered a small church in Overland Park, Kansas, that helped me begin to better understand who I was and helped me recognize my potential in life—not just my career. I was referred to the church by an extraordinary therapist with whom I was working at the time. Both this therapist and the minister at the church really believed in me. They saw my potential, recognized my gifts, and encouraged me to pursue a college degree.

Inspired and supported by these amazing women, I began what would become a lifelong spiritual practice, and I fully engaged in all the activities that this little church provided. I took classes, went to lectures, volunteered, and encouraged my friends to join me.

This next piece might sound crazy, but I swear it is true. When I was considering leaving my job and engaging in spiritual study and deeper self-reflection, I literally saw Jesus on my couch. In truth—and thankfully this was many, many moons ago—I was having an affair at the time. With a married man. Yeah, how screwed up was that? Not one of my proudest life achievements. Looking back, I can now recognize how insecure, unhappy, unfulfilled, and vulnerable I was. And, like so many of us, I made some bad decisions. This was a time in my life when I was really beginning to wake up to spirituality, and although I had intense chemistry with this man, I decided to end the relationship.

Not long after the breakup, this man came to my house, got down on his knees, and pleaded with me to take him back. I was confused, exhausted, and feeling really stuck. How could I tell him no? How could I hurt him? And then I looked to my right. There, sitting on the couch beside me, was Jesus. All I could think was, holy shit! Here is this guy groveling at my feet, pleading with me to take him back, and here's Jesus, with all his luminous beauty, assuring me that it is important to stay strong and end the relationship.

I get that it might be hard to fathom that Jesus Christ was sitting next to me. I truly get that. Yet, I also believe that when we are ready, the teacher will come. And for me, at that moment, it was literally Jesus.

The feeling of knowing that I was spiritually supported reassured me that I was on the right path—regardless of what other people thought. My own insecurities were holding me back. This experience reminded me that I was not alone, that I had never been alone, and that I never would be alone. I still think of that day with the assurance that I am always supported, and so are you. I trust that, with God—or whomever or whatever you believe in—all things are possible.

Courage also takes faith.

The next phase of my life was going to take great courage and faith indeed. It was going to take leading with the inherent guidance of my heart and trusting in the Divine path in order to cultivate and live a brave, bold, and beautiful life. I still employ courage every day. Acting courageously requires me to step into and live the truth, for as Eva Ritchey said, "Truth is the best arrow and courage the finest bow."[6]

Living Our Truth

It takes great courage to identify truth in life, explore what it means, and consider how truth and courage intersect in the way we show up in the world. In yogic philosophy, one of the Yamas (tenets to live by) is called Satya, which translates to "truthfulness." Practicing Satya means being truthful with our feelings, thoughts, words, and actions. It means being honest with ourselves and others.

In her fabulous book on yogic philosophy, *The Yamas & Niyamas: Exploring Yoga's Ethical Practice*, author Deborah Adele writes, "If we do not approach truth with our 'knees knocking', we have not really understood the profoundness of this guideline." She also explains in her chapter on Satya, in words that spoke directly to my heart, that "nice is an illusion, a cloak hiding lies."[7]

Nice. Having grown up as the "good girl," nice is something that I know well. It is something that I have been most of my life—often to a fault. This started to become apparent when I was working with Cathy Hawk, the founding director of Clarity International, a coaching and training firm that teaches skills for how to see, sense, and use energy as a primary life and work strategy. The work I was doing with Cathy had a lot to do with me feeling unseen, undervalued, and unappreciated by the people and teams with whom I was working at the time. During one session, I asked Cathy why she believed I was feeling this way. She told me I was too nice. My initial and obvious reaction was a resounding "What?!" I had always believed that being nice was a good thing! Then she explained that the problem was not that I *was* nice, but that I was always *acting* nice. At that moment, I felt confused because I did not fully understand what she meant.

Today, I get it. And there is nothing wrong with being nice. I am an inherently kind person. But "niceness" is not necessarily my "truth." As Adele explains, niceness is "an imposed image of what one thinks they should be. It is a packaging of self in a presentable box, imposed by an outer authority." In my case, this was the result of my childhood and upbringing.

Like so many of us, I faced challenges growing up. Early on in life, I was taught to believe it was scary to be bold. The youngest of two, I came from humble beginnings. There was a lot of chaos in my family, and I quickly learned that it was best to stay quiet, be nice, and just get things done. In order to stay "safe," I believed it was best to be "silent" and "good" to keep the waters calm in my turbulent home environment.

So many of the reactive behaviors that we learn in childhood that seem to keep us safe often fail us in adulthood. People who are conditioned to act "nice" hold a truth inside until they reach a breaking point and can become dangerously inappropriate, explosive, or act like a "crazy woman."

Have you ever, like me, lost it and thrown a plate at the wall in frustration? Have you also reached your limit, letting go of all passivity and becoming passive-aggressive (or just flat-out aggressive), and then felt awful about it after? Have you felt guilt, shame, and remorse because that is not how you want to show up in the world or with your friends and family?

All this happens because we are not living and speaking our truth. And failing to courageously live and speak our truth leads to suffering—suffering within ourselves and the suffering of others. On the flip side, the truth contains an incredible power to heal. It helps us increase our awareness, compassion for others, self-compassion, connection, and growth.

As Adele writes in her chapter on Satya, "Truth has the power to right wrongs and end sorrows. It is fierce in its demands and magnanimous in its offerings. It invites us to a place we rarely frequent and where we seldom know what the outcome will be." She continues by saying, "When we are real rather than nice, when we choose self-expression over self-indulgence, when we choose fluidity over rigidity, we begin to understand the deeper dynamics of truthfulness, and we begin to taste the freedom and goodness of this jewel."

Although it takes bravery to continue to show up in our lives with authenticity, vulnerability, and in our truth, being courageous often begins with small steps. And sometimes stretching ourselves and acting with more truth and courage can be done in just seconds.

Ninety Seconds of Insane Courage

In my personal life and with many clients, I use a practice called Ninety Seconds of Insane Courage. It was inspired in part by the 2011 movie *We Bought a Zoo* starring Matt Damon.[8] This heart-warming and touching film follows the journey of Benjamin Mee, a single father who moves his young children to the countryside to renovate and reopen a struggling zoo not long after his wife, the mother of his two children, dies. Toward the end of the movie, there is a scene in which Benjamin and his teenage son, Dylan, are sitting together on the ground with Spar, the zoo's seventeen-year-old tiger, who has become very sick. Benjamin asks Dylan what is going on between him and Lily, a girl Dylan had been spending a lot of time with before they had a falling out. Dylan admits to his dad that he really, really likes her and does not understand what has happened or what to do. He says, "You embarrass yourself if you say something, and you embarrass yourself if you don't." This causes Benjamin to smile and share these wise words with his son:

"Sometimes all you need is twenty seconds of insane courage. Just literally twenty seconds of just embarrassing bravery, and I promise you that something great will come of it."

And as is so often the case in movies, something great does come of it. Not long after talking with his dad, Dylan passes a sign in a window that says, "If you love me let me know." With rain coming down hard, he rushes to Lily's house and knocks on her window. When she opens it, he launches right into his twenty seconds of insane courage, saying, "Look, am I nuts to say that I missed you like crazy a lot? A lot?" He proceeds to tap into even more courage and get super vulnerable with her, words of pure authenticity pouring forth as rain pounds around him in classic Hollywood fashion. And then those beautiful and often-scary-to-say "I love you" words come out. Lily beams, and the two embrace.

While watching those scenes, a deep sense of awareness came over me and I, loving courage, started thinking about how long it would actually take to step into an uncomfortable thought, feeling, or experience and stay fully present.

Dr. Jill Bolte Taylor is a Harvard-trained, published neuroscientist. In 1996, she experienced a severe hemorrhage in the left hemisphere of her brain, causing her to lose the ability to walk, talk, read, and write. At that time, she could only access her brain's right hemisphere, where she describes "drifting in the peaceful consciousness where I lost all sense of urgency. Temporarily, my right brain existed solely in the present moment with no past regrets, present fears or future expectations."[9] Her memoir, *My Stroke of Insight*, which documents her experience with her stroke and her eight-year recovery, spent sixty-three weeks on the *New York Times* nonfiction bestseller list and is still routinely ranked as the number one book about strokes on Amazon.

In her latest book, *Whole Brain Living: The Anatomy of Choice and the Four Characters That Drive Our Life*, Taylor confirms what I intuitively knew to be true through my own work. Taylor writes that one of her most remarkable insights from her stroke and recovery was the realization that "We have the power to turn our emotional circuitry on and off by choice." She explains that "it takes less than 90 seconds for the chemistry of that emotion to flood through us and then flush completely out of our bloodstream. . . . Emotion only lasts in our bodies for about 90 seconds. After that, the physical reaction dissipates, UNLESS our cognitive brain kicks in and starts connecting our anger with past events."[10] She calls this the Ninety-Second Rule. Combining her work with my movie inspiration, I call it Ninety Seconds of Insane Courage.

Using Ninety Seconds of Insane Courage to Let Your Light Shine

From personal experience and through my work with hundreds of clients, I have seen the power of staying present to uncomfortable thoughts and emotions. It is simple but often not easy—especially at first. However, when you do not turn away from the discomfort, within ninety seconds or less, the intensity begins to dissipate. You may even feel a sense of relief, peace, or neutrality, which is a huge accomplishment if you were caught up in fear or anxiety just minutes before.

Today I use and teach this practice regularly. In my personal life, I have to stay present to unpleasant situations and feelings in and around me. This is especially true for experiences that leave me feeling particularly exposed or vulnerable. For the last six years, I have been a co-curator for our local TEDx Talks. The position fills me with great joy—it is such a privilege to work with smart, passionate women. And yet, after every live event, I routinely face my own insecurities. Like clockwork, I will start going over what I said onstage.

My internal dialogue usually goes something like this: "The only reason you got this opportunity is because you can financially support this cause. You are so stupid, and I cannot believe you said that onstage. Who do you think you are?"

Our inner critic can be ruthless and our worst enemy if we allow it to be. Especially when we put ourselves out into the world in a big way.

But thanks to my Ninety Seconds of Insane Courage practice, I have learned how to meet this moment and others like it. I can stop, pause for ninety seconds, and ask, *What is true here?* Some of what that voice says is true. I am privileged and able to support some causes and organizations I believe in. Yes, when I speak, I do not always speak formally. I love metaphors and can be a bit of a smartass. And then there's that question—*Who do you think you are?* Though said in my head with a snarky voice, the question becomes its own doorway.

Who am I?

I am reaching the end of my ninety seconds now, and the answer starts flowing in, not from a place of criticism but from a place of whole-hearted presence.

I am a very competent and accomplished woman. I have an advanced degree, have owned a successful business for many years, and have helped thousands of people through my counseling, coaching, and philanthropic work. I am passionate about women and women's issues. This commitment to and passion for supporting women personally, professionally, and systematically has driven my work for most of my life.

My advocacy work in the community and the legislature is important. It has included supporting women who seemingly did not have a voice. Through coaching, I have helped women develop the skills needed to testify on their own behalf and get the benefits they need to support themselves and their families. My values have always been aligned with supporting women and helping women to use their voices. Always.

The inner critic quiets down. The tension in my body fades, and I am left with the simplicity of breath moving in and out of my body. This process reminds me of one of my favorite writings by Marianne Williamson. In her book *A Return to Love: Reflections on the Principles of "A Course in Miracles,"* Williamson says, "Our deepest fear is not that we are inadequate. Our deepest fear is that we are powerful beyond measure. It is our light, not our darkness, that most frightens us. We ask ourselves, 'Who am I to be brilliant, gorgeous, talented, fabulous?' Actually, who are you not to be?"[11]

As I remember these words, I settle into my own inner knowing and a sense of profound peace.

It takes great heart to be fully expressed. It takes courage to use our voices. It requires vulnerability to be onstage, risking someone's ridicule, and to share our whole selves. And it takes all of that—heart, courage, and vulnerability—to shine our light and brilliance on a world and planet in desperate need of more light.

How can you let your light shine? How can you use your voice? How can you own your power? How do you align your values and use your talents to empower the world? How can your Ninety Seconds of Insane Courage practice help you rise more fully into the role you are being called to fill in the world?

The remainder of Marianne's quote says,

You are a child of God. You playing small does not serve the world. There is nothing enlightened about shrinking so that other people will not feel insecure around you. We are all meant to shine, as children do. We were born to make manifest the glory of God that is within us. It is not just in some of us; it is in everyone. And as we let our own light shine, we unconsciously give other people permission to do the same. As we are liberated from our own fear, our presence automatically liberates others.

With a practice like Ninety Seconds of Insane Courage, we can quiet the inner critic and own our beauty, power, and freedom of self-expression. Our talents are needed. It is important that we cultivate the right tools so that we can keep courageously showing up as the person we are meant to be in this world.

The Brave Beauty in Falling Down and Getting Back Up Again

I often think about what happens when we are not showing up courageously, doing our own work, sharing our stories, and allowing ourselves to shine brightly in the world. What happens when we feel too ashamed, frightened, or anxious to act with bravery? What happens when, for whatever reason, we are not getting down and dirty in "the arena" together?

"The arena" is a term Brené Brown explores in her *New York Times* bestseller *Daring Greatly: How the Courage to Be Vulnerable Transform the Way We Live, Love, Parent, and Lead*. The concept comes from Theodore Roosevelt's famous speech "Citizenship in a Republic," which he gave on April 23, 1910, in Paris, France. The speech is often referred to as "The Man in the Arena." A passage from Roosevelt's speech also led to Brown's utilization of the phrase "Daring Greatly" in the title of her book.

The speech was one of Roosevelt's most successful, and it is often quoted today. I find the message inspiring.

> It is not the critic who counts; not the man who points out how the strong man stumbles, or where the doer of deeds could have done them better. The credit belongs to the man who is actually in the arena, whose face is marred by dust and sweat and blood; who strive valiantly; who errs, who comes short again and again, because there is no effort without error and shortcoming; but who does actually strive to do the deeds; who knows great enthusiasms, the great devotions; who spends himself in a worthy cause; who at the best knows in the end the triumph of high achievement, and who at the worst, if he fails, at least fails while daring greatly, so that his place shall never be with those cold and timid souls who neither know victory nor defeat.[12]

If that is not a speech about courage, I do not know what is!

I love Brown's inspiration she took from Theodore Roosevelt's speech. She writes in her own fierce way that "If you are not in the arena also getting your ass kicked, I am not interested in your feedback."[13] Sometimes our courage is threatened by other people. We fear standing out as different, or we concern ourselves with what others might say or think about our actions. But the truth is that the only one who stands in the way of your courage is you. Theodore's wife, Eleanor Roosevelt, said, "You gain strength, courage and confidence by every experience in which you stop to look fear in the face. . . . You must do the thing which you think you cannot do."[14]

Do not let other people's ideas of what is possible stand in your way. If someone else is not in the arena, showing up again and again even after they get kicked in the face, they do not deserve to give you feedback. And the opposite is also true—when someone *is* in the arena and they see the potential in you, it is important to listen.

Saying "Yes" to Your Highest Potential Takes Courage

As a co-curator for TEDxCherryCreekWomen, I have had the honor of working with hundreds of women, offering them the emotional support and coaching that is often necessary to help them get up onto that big TEDx stage in front of hundreds of people, speak from their hearts, and tell their stories. It is an unbelievable experience to watch these women walk bravely onto the stage. They spark and inspire deep conversations and connections through their courage, their vulnerability, their willingness to be seen, and the amazing work they have done to turn trauma into triumph, grief into gratitude, and obstacles into opportunities. Each woman comes to the stage with an idea worth spreading, which is the core of what TED is about.

I was introduced to the TEDx community through TEDxCrestmoorParkWomen, which would soon evolve into TEDxCherryCreekWomen. It was a joyful, albeit slightly terrifying, beginning. In 2015, I noticed women in my community doing exceptional work. One had just written and published a powerful book detailing her own personal experience of grief and trauma. Another friend was making and producing a movie. A client of mine had recently journeyed to all fifty states, interviewing people in their communities who were making a difference, and she was working through writer's block and the challenges that can—and certainly do—arise when getting a book published. I had also been published that year, and meeting that milestone created the momentum and drive to go even bigger and do even more to serve. I intuitively knew that something needed to happen to bring these incredible women and others in the community together. Being the connector that I am, I invited a handful of women over to my home. In my backyard, I explained that I felt a collective energy between us all and a sense that we were meant to collaborate and create something impactful.

During the meeting, Dafna Michaelson Jenet, our TEDxCherryCreekWomen founder, blurted out that she had a TEDx license.

Dafna—who firmly believes in her driving mantra of not complaining about a problem without working on the solution—had applied for a TEDx license when she lived in Denver's Crestmoor Park neighborhood. She had a vision of bringing women's voices from the Rocky Mountain region to the TEDx stage. Actually, she had given her own TEDx Talk and had been asked to be on the selection committee for another independent event. When only white males were chosen to speak, she decided to request an all-women event, which was met with a "no." What she did not know was that TED was about to launch TEDWomen. Just a few weeks later, they contacted her and asked her to apply. She was awarded the first TEDxWomen license in the state of Colorado. From there, Dafna and her husband built TEDxCrestmoorParkWomen.

That day in my backyard, we decided to move forward with the TEDx event. I spoke in 2016. When Dafna initially asked me to speak, my first response was a resounding "No way!" I had grown up with a lot of trauma, like so many of us, and it takes enormous courage and vulnerability to share our fragile life stories. It was even more terrifying to consider sharing those stories on a stage in front of hundreds, and even thousands, of people. But then I started thinking about how inspired I was—and still am—by the women I see every day really putting themselves out there.

I was reminded of Geneen Roth in her book *Women, Food, and God: An Unexpected Path to Almost Everything*. She was courageous enough to share that some days when her husband left for work, she secretly hoped that he would die and never come home. Of course, she did not really want him to die, but I do think that she was authentic in not wanting him to come home. Although dark, it made me laugh. How many of us have had dark thoughts yet felt too afraid to share them? And then there are writers like Elizabeth Gilbert, Cheryl Strayed, Rachel Hollis, Glennon Doyle, Anne Lamott, Gabby Bernstein, and so many others who have courageously shared their stories, connecting with women all over the world. Every one of us has our stories, but far too many of us keep them hidden, feeling alone and often clothed in shame.

The thing is, no matter how perfect our lives might look on the outside (and we all know how much upkeep that can take), there is beauty in being raw. And so, quaking in my ruby red cowboy boots—literally—I called on my inner Cowardly Lion, took to the TEDxCrestmoorParkWomen stage, and gave a talk on "The Illusion of Perfection" (more about that later!).

Once I mustered the courage to give my talk and share in the TEDxWomen experience, I realized how empowering and meaningful it was, not just for me, but for all the women who shared their ideas that day. We led each other to the stage and to that moment of showing up for our highest potential. Our mutual support and care as we walked the path of courage were far more meaningful and impactful to me than the talk itself. We all walked away knowing we had felt our fear and did it anyway!

TEDx Feature: Pat Jacques, "What If Everything About Me Is Inherently Right?"

When I think about courage, feeling fearful, and doing it anyway, I am often reminded of a talk given by Pat Jacques, a bold and brave woman who took the TEDxCherryCreekWomen stage in 2018. I had known Pat for many years and was blessed to support her on her journey. Pat's talk, entitled "What If Everything About

Me Is Inherently Right?", explored what she believed it meant to be a woman based on what her family and society taught her . . . and what it was like to completely change that definition for her own well-being.

I especially love the summary of Pat's talk, provided by TEDxCherryCreekWomen.

> If we could only use one word to describe Pat Jacques, that word would be BADASS! She is one of the most courageous and authentic people who shines her bright light and inspires others to shine theirs. She is vibrant and energetic. And her belly laugh is infectious and contagious. This is all especially remarkable, given her early life of violence and abuse. Here she shares her story and transformation to understand that everything about her, and you, is inherently right. [15]

Right out of the gate, Pat took over the TEDxCherryCreek-Women stage and captivated the audience with her courage, energy, and sincere expression. She shared that she struggled with her weight since childhood, realized in her teens that she was gay, was drawn to motocross from a very early age—an activity that was "too rough" for girls—and struggled with shame and guilt for a good part of her life. She vulnerably shared that as a teenager, on top of undergoing weekly "weigh-ins" and dietary restrictions, the last thing she wanted to be was gay. Years later, still trying to prove to herself and others that she was "straight," she suffered a violent sexual assault, which left her with even more shame and guilt. Like so many other women, she believed the assault was her fault.

A smart and technologically savvy woman, Pat later started her own tech business, which quickly flourished. On the outside, Pat looked successful and happy. On the inside, she hated herself and her life and lived in constant pain. During those dark years, Pat chose to believe that she was ugly, that no one could ever really love her, and that she was an abomination.

Pat eventually went to therapy and found healing, realizing that she had made herself both a prisoner and her own personal jailer. She also realized that there were thousands, if not millions, of other women out there who felt as she did—that something was inherently wrong with them. When she Googled the term "inherently wrong," definitions such as "bad seed" and "permanently flawed" showed up. When she Googled "inherently right," most of what came up consisted of political references. It occurred to her in that moment to ask these questions:

- What if everything about me is inherently right?
- What if I can see the best in me, even when I am not at my best?
- What if I am supposed to be racing motocross, jumping across a gully—the sport I watched and loved so many years earlier but was told was too dangerous for girls?
- What if I am supposed to love everyone—especially women?

I adore Pat, and I especially love her story. She is the walking embodiment of courage. She bravely and vulnerably shares her experience with body image issues, her sexuality, using her voice, and following her heart. And she is a total badass, teaching women all over the country to bravely face their fears, get on a motorcycle, and unleash the innate power that lives within each of us.

Pat left her audience with a final question: "What would your life look like, who would you be, how would you show up if you knew—I mean really knew—that everything about you is inherently right?"

Face the World with Courage

As Pat's story demonstrates, it takes courage to leave relationships, jobs, ingrained patterns, and what may feel safe but does not serve us, in search of what really makes us come alive. It takes courage to have faith in Spirit, our hearts, and ourselves. It takes courage to be vulnerable, yet, in doing so, we create space for others to step into their vulnerability, too. As I said at the beginning of this chapter, some days it takes courage to just get out of bed and step into the world.

We are all wounded in some way, and no one has a "perfect" life, yet I firmly believe that we are much stronger together and that, as women, we are capable of climbing and reaching high peaks. I also firmly believe that we are much stronger than we think. We just need to employ the courage of the Lion and be brave enough to fully love ourselves and show up as our biggest, boldest, and most beautiful selves.

The world needs all of us to share our gifts and talents. Doing so is scary, for sure. I certainly have walked that teetering path, quaking in my ruby red cowboy boots in search of the Land of Oz and the Wonderful Wizard. In doing so—in being brave enough to listen to my heart and trust the Divine journey—I have lived, learned, and witnessed through my own experiences and the powerful stories of other women what happens when we get into the arena, take to the stage, live our truth, use our voices, and authentically and courageously connect.

The Practice: Ninety Seconds of Insane Courage

The next time you feel triggered by an uncomfortable wave of thoughts, feelings, or emotions, I invite you to lean into it rather than resist it, as most of us are consciously and subconsciously conditioned to do. Allow the discomfort to fully arise and take ninety seconds to be fully present with what you are feeling. See, sense, or feel where this energy is located in your body. Put your hand on that spot. Allow the feeling to be there, even if doing so initially makes you want to throw up or crawl out of your skin.

My experiences, science, and even Matt Damon know it only takes a few seconds to release the energy of uncomfortable emotions and to be able to step more fully into our hearts and our true desires.

Stepping into your Ninety Seconds of Insane Courage over and over again can create new neural pathways and rewire your brain. The Ninety Seconds of Insane Courage technique can change the game of your life. Practicing it regularly shifts the ways we have been conditioned to react into opportunities to respond. When we stay present, slow things down, truly feel our feelings, and trust our hearts, we can create extraordinary transformation in both our internal and external worlds. And it all starts with courage.

Oh God of Second Chances, may I have the courage to stay present, listen to my heart, and trust the Divine path.

2

Leading with the Heart

I shall take the heart. For brains do not make one hap-
py, and happiness is the best thing in the world.
—L. Frank Baum, *The Wonderful Wizard of Oz*

Rational thinking did not get me where I am today. My heart did. If I had allowed my mind to rule, fear would have won. From the beginning, I knew there was something more for me in this life and that leading from my heart would allow me to live a life of courage, love, and truth. That said, being a heart person was not and is not always easy. It can be painful, overwhelming, and confusing. But allowing our heart's longing to lead puts us on our soul's path, which is a path that ultimately leads to joy. Our hearts know exactly what we need, want, and desire, whereas the mind and its propensity for overthinking and overidentification with intellect often leads us astray and causes us to feel stressed, depressed, and underexpressed. The heart, though, knows. It just knows . . .

I have known for many years now that I am an old soul empath who absorbs the emotion of those around me. I think I came into this world consciously aware, knowing that I was being guided by my heart and a power greater than just me—although that realization did not really stick until early in my adult life. I remember one of the first times I allowed my heart to take the lead over my rational mind in a professional context. I was in my early twenties, working in advertising, on the fast track to success. Our agency was trying to win a major client, and the account executive assigned to the project was not doing well. Although I was young and still green in the industry, my boss asked me to take over and meet with the prospect's VP of marketing. When I entered the meeting, I was nervous and had little idea what I was doing or what I was going to say. Instead of trying to pretend that I did, my heart told me to be vulnerable and to ask this VP of marketing to help me. He laughed, yet he connected with that authenticity and appreciated my realness and vulnerability. Leading from the heart, connecting with this innate intuition, and allowing myself to be in a place of not knowing turned into a $1.6 million contract for my agency.

Relying on our hearts and trusting our intuition is inherently simple, and maybe, in part, it is that simplicity that stands in the way of most people living joyful lives. Remaining overly identified with our intellect—what we think we know—is what makes many of us believe that we are keeping ourselves safe. And, let us face it, most of us are living in this socialized place of "safety." However, there are so many opportunities to ascend by tapping into our hearts, which helps us learn—and lean more fully into—who we innately are.

Me, I am a total heart-soaked sponge.

Bricks and Sponges

Many years ago, I took my son to see an energy healer. The healer asked my son to consider what happens when you drop a brick into a bucket of water versus when you drop a sponge into the same bucket. My son very quickly described how the brick would make a splash and sink to the bottom of the bucket. The sponge, however, would soak up the water and then sink. "You are a sponge," she told my son.

There are brick people, and there are sponge people, just as there are head people and heart people. Head people tend to be highly rational, practical, and logical in their functioning, and they often operate like bricks—solid, strong, rigid, and mostly set in their ways. They make a splash, which may displace the water around them, and move forward seemingly unscathed. And then there are heart people who lead from a place of intuition, compassion, vulnerability, and love, but risk absorbing too much and sinking down, or drying out from over-giving.

Then there are sponges who try to act like bricks, which can feel awful and awkward. It is very confusing to try to behave like a brick when you are innately a sponge. We sponges wonder why we can't seem to feel good about our world and lives; we possess a deep knowing that there is something more in this life. It is hard to be a sponge in a world built for bricks, and denying our softness, flexibility, vulnerability, and empathic nature can deplete our worth and well-being.

Here is a story that I wrote years ago that illuminates what happens when a sponge tries to lead from her head versus her heart. And, yes, this is based on a true and very personal story . . .

One day a beautiful sponge met a brick—a strong, firm, and successful brick. Sponge loved Brick's looks, smarts, wit, and success in the world of tall buildings and hard things. Brick loved Sponge's softness, flexibility, and ability to absorb the world around her. They made good companions—the strong, resilient brick and the soft, absorbent sponge.

Then life started happening. There were many sunny days when Brick and Sponge did just fine. However, as time went on, Sponge started to feel a bit brittle from too much heat and not enough moisture. Brick—well, he was a brick, in sunshine or in rain. The rainy days were also hard for Sponge. Brick continued to do well, even seeming to thrive, built solid in his brickness, while Sponge often got left out in the rain.

The rain started to saturate Sponge. She became heavy and unable to absorb more. Brick, being a brick, did not recognize her oversaturation and continued in his brickness, unaware of Sponge's challenges. But Brick tried. He tried all his hard, solid brick tactics to get Sponge to become a brick because that was all he knew. He sat on her, he squished her, and he got mad and frustrated with Sponge when his brick ways just added more heaviness to her. She simply could not absorb more. Eventually, Brick withdrew. He decided that Brick Land was where he belonged and spent more and more time there.

Sponge felt sad and tried all the ways she could think of to feel better. But she just got heavier and squishier until one day, she decided to just be still and lay in the sun. Suddenly, she realized that the warmth and energy of the sun were absorbing the heaviness, and, bit by bit, she became lighter and lighter. Sponge decided to take herself into the sun daily and let it evaporate the excess weight she had been carrying. She started feeling better and more like herself as she became increasingly buoyant and strong. Sponge realized that the way she had been feeling really had nothing to do with Brick. She had forgotten to allow the sun to do what the sun does. She also now understood that it never rains forever—that if she got caught in the rain, eventually the sun would be back and continue to do its glorious sun thing. She even realized that she could wring herself out, release the heaviness all by herself, get back up, and become a more beautiful sponge every day.

As Sponge started to share her new knowledge with Brick, she recognized that Brick had more pores than she originally thought. The little holes in his core were similar to hers. She realized that although he was a brick and would never be a sponge and that she was a sponge and would never be a brick, she could share the things she absorbed, because her heaviness was not as heavy for him. Sponge also came to understand that being a brick is not easy. Bricks need the softness of a sponge. Sponge's big heart softened Brick's hard exterior. They found a way to live together, appreciating and supporting their differences and finding beauty in each other.

The Head and the Heart in a Land of Bricks

Let us face it—we live in a world of bricks. The bricks of buildings, the bricks of walls, and the bricks of our socialized cognitive conditioning. As human beings, we are taught from the onset to "think" our way through life, an approach that is reinforced every day through conversations, internal dialogue, and omnipresent media messages. We are constantly bombarded with messages such as "What were you thinking? Where is your brain? Use your head."

And that is the thing: our brains are hard-wired to be thinking machines. Due to socialized conditioning and cognitive development, our brains are constantly working to solve, resolve, and create. However, the brain is just a subtotal of all the data it has collected up to a certain point in time. Like a computer, the brain receives data and regurgitates it back. It has a very useful job and helps us continually push forward, yet it can also hold us back.

Decades of scientific research have found that most of our thoughts are negative. The numbers vary, but it is commonly believed that we have somewhere between 60,000 and 70,000 thoughts per day. Of those thoughts, the majority are repetitive and critical. Dr. Rick Hanson, PhD psychologist and Senior Fellow of UC Berkeley's

Greater Good Science Center, explains that we are hard-wired to think negatively.[1] According to Hanson and others who are actively studying the brain and how we think, humans have evolved to be fearful. Our brains trick us so that we overestimate threats, underestimate opportunities, and underestimate the resources we have available for dealing with threats and fulfilling opportunities. Feelings of fight, flight, or freeze, which once protected our ancestors from the threats of lions, tigers, and bears, have most of us living in a whirlwind of anxiety and seemingly nonstop negative thoughts that keep us from our highest self. As Don Miguel Ruiz, spiritual teacher and bestselling author of *The Four Agreements: A Practical Guide to Personal Freedom*, says, "Ninety-five percent of the beliefs we have stored in our minds are nothing but lies, and we suffer because we believe all these lies."[2]

But what if it does not have to be this way?

In his profound article "Your Mind: Friend or Foe," American author and Buddhist teacher Jack Kornfield writes, "My teacher Sri Nisargadatta explained it like this: 'The mind creates the abyss, and the heart crosses it.' When you rest in the present moment with mindfulness, you open to a presence which is timeless and beyond the understanding of thought. It is by returning to the awareness beyond thoughts that you experience real healing. When your mind and heart open, you realize who you are, the timeless, limitless awareness behind all thought."[3] I cannot think of a better way to put it. We need our hearts to help us cross the abysses in our lives and return to our vast true nature.

The Wisdom of the Body

You have probably had a gut feeling about something before or felt butterflies in your stomach, innately knowing that something was so very right or so very wrong. This intuition, which is defined as "a natural ability or power that makes it possible to know some-thing without any proof or evidence,"[4] has often been referred to as instinct, a sixth sense, divination, clairvoyance, and even extrasen-sory perception (ESP). Yet so many of us ignore our intuition. We rely on our thinking rather than tapping into our innate knowing, refusing to allow ourselves to be led by gut feelings. When we dig below the surface, we learn that a lot of this conditioning begins in childhood. While our brains are still developing in childhood, we tend to lead from our heart, gut, and impulses—until we are taught otherwise.

As an example, my older brother, Mike, was incredibly impulsive when we were growing up. Mike struggled with ADHD, which was not well understood back in the '60s, but he certainly tapped into his creative impulses. He did the craziest stuff, like finding paint in the garage and deciding to spray paint the house next door because it was white, and he believed that it should be more colorful. Then there was the time when my mom had a crate of grapefruits delivered to our home, and they were left in the living room. Mike saw the grapefruits and decided that they looked like baseballs, so he started throwing them at the living room wall. He had very creative—and not always appropriate—impulses, which we all have, though we tend to ignore or suppress them. Yet, when we are young, we have these inspired ways of wanting to express ourselves. This unique creativity—the expression of our unique gifts and our innate sense of intuition—is something beautiful that so many of us were punished or made to feel wrong for. Right or wrong, it is the punishment or judgment of our impulses that shuts down our creativity. It creates the feeling that our innate instincts are wrong.

We then feel guilt or shame. Our thinking brains kick in, and we believe that because someone is mad, we must have done something wrong. If that happens enough times, we start to internalize the belief that there must be something fundamentally wrong with us when we live our essence. When we experience judgment from the adults in our lives, we begin to repress our intuitive impulses. Although my brother's behaviors were extreme, and his struggles with ADHD were not understood or treated until later in his life, the fear of punishment causes most of us to mistrust our own innate creativity.

When we stop trusting the flow of our intuition and our deep sense of connection to the Divine in all things, including ourselves, we stop allowing ourselves to innately know what wants to come through us. We ignore our gut instincts, even though they are sometimes screaming at us to listen. Think about your children if you have kids. Parents know when something is up. We just know. There is a physicality to it. There is a place in the body where it settles. There is a "knowing" to it that is not based within the mind. It is in the gut.

According to Indian American author and alternative medicine advocate Deepak Chopra, "Intuitive skills are inside of all of us. Intuition is always there for us, to guide, protect, and help us develop. As we grow into adulthood, we may push this intuition to the side to conform to what society says we should do. The more we do this, the less we tend to listen to that little voice or those gut feelings."[5]

And the less we listen, the less we live from our true selves.

Living from the Heart

Most people lead with their brains. Some people have learned to lead from their guts. I have always been led by (and believed in) the inherent wisdom of the heart.

The heart is powerful and all-knowing. I have been heart-focused since an early age, able to feel the energy and intuition of my heart. When I have leaned into and been led by my heart, I have never been steered wrong. It has been through listening to my heart, rather than relying on cognitive intelligence or society, which has led to many of the most incredible experiences of my life. And it is not for lack of intelligence; I am. Like so many women, I am and have always been blessed with the high intellectual capacity necessary to work through challenges using logic. But it has always been through tapping into my heart and other parts of my body and connecting to Source that I have found more profound guidance, insight, and wisdom.

It was my heart that knew it was time to leave a successful job to pursue a passion for service and social work, even when friends and family thought I was crazy. It was my heart that knew it was time for me to move across the country. It is through the heart that I have tapped into intuition, implemented new ideas, and inherently identified the people with whom I was supposed to connect. For decades now, I have engaged in the practice of asking my heart questions versus asking my head, which just regurgitates data or elicits fear. While my brain goes over a question or an idea, trying to rationalize and sort through the information filed there, my heart always knows the answer before I even get the question out. Some call this intuition. Others call it a connection with Source. For me, it is both. Tapping into the heart allows Source energy (God, the Divine, etc.) to come through us, to guide us, to be with us. Science would call this coherence. According to HeartMath Institute Research Director Dr. Rollin McCraty, "Coherence is the state when the heart, mind, and emotions are in energetic alignment and cooperation. It is a state that builds resilience—personal energy is accumulated, not wasted—leaving more energy to manifest intentions and harmonious outcomes."[6]

The Science Behind the Heart

While shifting out of predominantly clinical work as a social worker and into more somatic and energetic patterning work, I became curious about the science behind what I had always innately known to be true—that the heart is as intelligent, if not more intelligent, than the brain. For decades, scientists and researchers have been making discoveries and advancing our understanding of the neurological patterns of the brain, so why not the heart too? With my inner nerd in high gear, I began looking for proof in the form of scientific data to validate these truths, which led me to the Institute of HeartMath, a not-for-profit research and educational organization. With almost three decades of scientifically validated research, they have demonstrated that not only the brain, but the heart itself, is an intelligent bodily system.

I am admittedly not the most tech-savvy person in the world. I tend to break technology. Even so, I had this awareness that when it came to measuring the energetic fields of the body, technology could help. At my first HeartMath workshop, I watched the facilitator, Greg Bradden, put the emWave2 on a volunteer. The emWave2 is a Bluetooth device designed to help people shift their emotional state in real-time, allowing them to think more clearly and feel better. It analyzes heart rhythms, which are measured by heart wave variability (HWV), and indicates how emotional states affect the nervous system. This innovative technology measures HWV and offers a unique window into the quality of the communication between the heart and the brain, which directly impacts how we feel and perform in life.

As the small heart monitor, connected to Bluetooth, was placed on the volunteer's ear, I could see her heart rhythm displayed on the large screens in the room. The images were drastically different when the volunteer focused on love, gratitude, and appreciation versus when she focused on something that caused her to feel frustrated and stressed.

When we are stressed, we feel poorly, and our brain functioning and creative thinking become impaired. We can overlook or forget important details, overreact to the small stuff, say things we inevitably regret, feel overwhelmed, have trouble sleeping, and feel exhausted and drained.

But what if it does not need to be this way?

The emWave2 has helped me and many of my clients learn how to regulate and restore emotional balance in the present moment. It helps to synchronize the heart, mind, and body—allowing whoever is using this technology to reset and cultivate composure and inner clarity while calming reactive emotions and neutralizing stress.

HeartMath has recorded that the heart is roughly sixty times greater electrically and up to 5,000 times stronger magnetically than the brain.[7] Essentially, these revolutionary findings have shown that the brain is relatively weak in comparison to the heart. The science uncovered through HeartMath is constantly demonstrating that there is, at the very least, two-way communication between the heart and the brain. Although most people have been taught to believe that it is the brain that leads the heart, it is actually a joint effort, and the brain is just as likely to be influenced by the heart. This quote from HeartMath sums it up:

Most of us have been taught in school that the heart is constantly responding to "orders" sent by the brain in the form of neural signals. However, it is not as commonly known that the heart actually sends more signals to the brain than the brain sends to the heart! Moreover, these heart signals have a significant effect on brain function—influencing emotional processing as well as higher cognitive faculties such as attention, perception, memory, and problem-solving. In other words, not only does the heart respond to the brain, but the brain continuously responds to the heart.[8]

Studying HeartMath's research was this great "aha" moment for me, scientifically validating what I had known to be true. I loved that what was considered "woo-woo" by many back in the 1980s was now being demonstrated to me visually and backed by decades of scientific research.

By focusing only on the thoughts in our heads, we sacrifice so much of the information that is available to us. This overreliance on thinking also keeps us from feeling, which taps into the root of most of our common problems. Most of us are conditioned to value thinking over feeling. But, in my decades of living, loving, falling down, and getting back up again, I have learned that the heart is at the center of living a connected, authentic, empowered, and fully courageous life. Our hearts know how to communicate and connect through radical vulnerability. It is through courageously leading from the heart that we are able to live our most authentic lives and express our whole, perfect, and complete selves in the world.

TEDx Feature: Phoenix Jackson, "The Spirit of the Moment"

When I think of someone who truly and courageously leads from her heart, my thoughts immediately go to Phoenix Jackson. Phoenix is a young, vibrant woman of color. Phoenix and I met when both of us served on the board of directors of the Carson J. Spencer Foundation, a not-for-profit organization focused on suicide prevention, with a primary focus on men and youth. I was immediately drawn to Phoenix—a young and beautiful woman— and we quickly developed a strong connection. Not long after we met, Phoenix, who is an excellent marketer, supported me with my branding and website. I then began coaching her through a career change, relationship challenges, and many of the other inevitable life circumstances that we all face as we evolve and develop into our greater, most authentic selves.

When I entered the TEDx world and decided to speak that first year, our team felt that Phoenix—given her potency, multiple gifts and talents, creative spark, and huge heart—should take to the stage. Her TEDxCrestmoorParkWomen talk, "The Spirit of the Moment," was one of the most creative, authentic, and inspiring talks I heard that year. And that is saying a lot, as she was in great company. Her talk, which both started and finished with the heart, truly touched my heart and those of so many others in the crowded theater that day.

True to Phoenix's nature, she began her talk by asking everyone in the audience to take a moment to put their hands over their hearts, explaining that our heartbeat is the very first thing that we hear in the womb and the first movement that happens eighteen days after conception. She expressed that hers was beating fast, an embodiment of her nervousness and excitement about being on stage speaking to a TEDx audience. She also said that it signaled her beautiful aliveness. She then continued to talk about how powerful and all-knowing the heart is, sharing that most of us never stop to listen to it. More than that, we never stop to listen to the heart in the moment.

Phoenix went on to tell a beautiful story about her introduction to African dance, which would eventually lead her into an extraordinary adventure and a life of service that still inspires her and the lives she touches today. Although she had no background in dance, and she was fearful of trying something new, she felt called to move. At nineteen years old, with her infant son strapped on her back, Phoenix attended her first dance class with a troupe of women from all around the world who had been dancing together for years. And it turned out that she was quite good!

Not long after Phoenix began dancing, she performed a solo piece at a festival with the same troupe of women. During the festival, a well-known teacher approached Phoenix and asked her to choreograph an African dance piece for an international audience. Suddenly, there was that quick beat of Phoenix's heart again. She had never taught a class, let alone choreographed anything before. Scared and nervous, she decided to move through the fear and trepidation and do it anyway, expressing that she felt present enough to feel her heartbeat, listen to her heart in the moment, and know that this was the right path. And it was. Her first choreographed piece was a great success.

Sometime later, a woman approached Phoenix, offering to help her refine her talent. This woman taught Phoenix everything that she knew, and she encouraged her to leave the States and begin teaching her class. Astounded, Phoenix was suddenly teaching some of the very same women who, just a few years before, she had learned to dance from and with. With expressed humility, she shared that she could not understand how she had transitioned from student to teacher or why these women wanted to learn from her. All she knew was that she was called to move, that she wanted to dance.

From that class, Phoenix created something even more beautiful. She transformed the class into Dance to Live Health, an initiative based on a curriculum she created that focused on women's health, including movement, mental health and wellness, and nutrition. And then, in what felt like an overnight development, she was contacted by her alma mater, the University of Denver (DU). They had heard about her curriculum and felt that they needed the substance of it—that they needed her—as part of their women's college program. There went the quick thump, thump, thump of her heart, and she once again followed its wisdom. At twenty-six years old, Phoenix became the youngest faculty member and one of the few members of color at DU. And all of this because, years before, she had listened to her heart's calling to move, faced her fear of trying something new, strapped her baby to her back, and danced!

Phoenix's story illuminates how we can all learn from and inspire each other. It illuminates the extraordinary opportunities that open up for us when we listen to, lead from, and follow the wisdom of our hearts. When I think of Phoenix, I am always reminded to slow down, be with the moment, and listen to my heart. She reminds me that the heart always knows.

Phoenix closed her TEDxCrestmoorParkWomen talk by asking everyone in the audience to stand up and once again put their hands over their hearts. She invited everyone to join her in repeating what she called "A Pledge of Allegiance to Ourselves."

It went like this:

"I pledge to stop the distractions of my life, to listen to myself, my true inner wants, my desires, my needs, and what it is that will fill me. I vow to trust myself and to trust the journey."

It is in trusting ourselves and the journey that we find the destiny of our lives. It is the heart, not the intellect, which knows the path. The desires of your heart are the calling of your future.

Have faith, and let your heart be your guide. You are what you have been waiting for. It is all inside of you. I promise.

The Practice: A Heart-Centered Practice to Develop a Sense of Calmness, Coherence, and Clarity

Here is a HeartMath technique called Heart Lock-In. It is a heart-centered practice that can be done anytime, anywhere. This practice is great for when you are lost in your thinking mind, wondering about the answer to a big question or asking what you should do next with your life. When you get caught up in spiraling thoughts, this simple, quick technique can help you find your heart and reestablish your center.

To begin, close your eyes if you are comfortable doing so, and start breathing into your heart, almost as if your heart is breathing you. Breathe into your heart-center for a count of three and then breathe out for a count of three, finding your own personal rhythm.

Once you feel settled in your breathing, drop into your heart. Ask your heart what you need to know, or think of the question you are pondering at this moment. And listen. Listen to the intuitive power of your heart and its great intelligence.

The heart always answers instantly. Sometimes it answers even before you ask for guidance.

When you are ready, open your eyes. Ask yourself if you got an answer from your heart. How do you feel now?

Messages from the heart come in many different forms. As your heart communicates, I encourage you to trust what you hear and feel. Be with each moment as it comes, allowing the heart's message to arise without projecting into the future, which is the thinking that creates anxiety and angst. When you are in a place of love and gratitude, you are best positioned to create coherence between your head and your heart.

The Heart Lock-In technique is designed to provide you with greater clarity—if you allow for and trust it. It helps to calm the mind and balance emotions, and it helps you to do so with creativity.

Ask your heart, and your heart will answer. Trust it. Play with it. Practice connecting with it. I do this practice almost every morning during ME (My Essence) time. Reflect on your heart, follow your intuition, and see how it feels. Notice where it leads you on the yellow brick road of personal curiosity, embodied power, and discovery. You may find yourself making decisions that feel more authentic and lead to more positivity, growth, and joy.

I invite you to call on your inner Mike, who, with unbounded creativity and joy, throws paint and grapefruits at white walls. I invite you to call on your inner Phoenix, who, with a baby on her back, lets fear fall to the floor and follows her heart's desire to dance. I invite you to trust the calling and truth of your heart and follow where it leads. Step in and trust the desires of your heart.

Oh God of Second Chances, may I follow my heart with creativity, joy, and trust.

3

Come to the Edge

"Come to the edge," he said.
"We, we are afraid!" they responded.
"Come to the edge," he said.
"We can't, we will fall!" they responded.
"Come to the edge," he said.
And so, they came.
And he pushed them.
And they flew.
—Guillaume Apollinaire

This short poem by Guillaume Apollinaire is one of my all-time favorites.[1] Every time I read it, I am reminded that we are all afraid of uncertainty and the unknown. We are also often scared to be seen and to courageously connect with others—sometimes even with ourselves. It takes courage to come to the edge—to take risks, to be vulnerable, to allow ourselves to be truly seen as we are.

Brené Brown has done a lot of work on vulnerability—what it is, why it is important, and how we can cultivate it for whole-hearted living. You will notice that these subjects start to overlap. Courage, being heart-centered, and vulnerability are all connected. As Brown writes, "You cannot get to courage unless you walk through vulnerability."[2] She also says, "Vulnerability is the birthplace of love, belonging, joy, courage and creativity. It is the source of hope, empathy, accountability and authenticity."[3]

But despite its many benefits, vulnerability is not easy for most of us. I have often felt ashamed of the vulnerabilities in my life. For a long time, I did not like telling people about my family of origin or the circumstances of my life when I was growing up. I feared their judgment. Worse, I feared that those stories represented who I was and that my own self-judgment would swallow me whole.

Something powerful happens when we truly claim who we are. We stop pretending. We stop putting on masks and facades. We allow ourselves to simply *be*, and it is often in that being that we can fully step into our purpose. Or, as Brown puts it, "If we want to live and love with our whole hearts, and if we want to engage with the world from a place of worthiness, we have to talk about the things that get in the way—especially shame, fear and vulnerability."[4] This is how we walk to the edge and fly—by embracing our whole selves, even the parts that are hard to look at. And for me, that means learning to own my story, claiming it for myself, and even rewriting the ending.

The Power of Owning Your Story

It is impossible to heal without vulnerably sharing ourselves with the world. We cannot pretend away our hurt, pain, regret, blame, shame, or sadness, although we might try.

For me, stories are one of the most powerful medicines. You do not have to share your story publicly, like in a book. Whether with a supportive friend, family member, or therapist, we all need people who will listen. Life is often too big for any one person to hold. We all encounter different forms of trauma. As social creatures, we are not meant to wade through it all by ourselves.

I have learned this time and again in my own life. For many years, I tried to stuff my stories way down, but when I did that, I never felt whole. It was like I was cutting off parts of myself because I did not know how to integrate them. After decades of work, I have come a long way. My stories and vulnerabilities are now part of my power. No matter the difficulties I face, I can trust that I have walked through challenges and have emerged on the other side stronger for it.

I am choosing to share some of my life stories in this book because I want you to know that you are not alone. Our vulnerability not only helps us, but it also has the power to support others in their healing process. In the introduction to her book *Daring Greatly: How the Courage to Be Vulnerable Transforms the Way We Live, Love, Parent, and Lead*, Brené Brown writes, "Vulnerability is not a weakness, and the uncertainty, risk and emotional exposure we face every day are not optional. Our only choice is a question of engagement. Our willingness to own and engage with our vulnerability determines the depth of our courage and the clarity of our purpose; the level to which we protect ourselves from being vulnerable is a measure of our fear and disconnection."[5]

As I share my stories from growing up, I hope that you too will have the courage to willingly engage with your vulnerability and know that it is a sign of your great courage.

An Upbringing of Love and Difficulty

My father struggled with depression, something that I was unaware of until his first attempt to take his life when I was ten years old. Mom worked nights, so Dad was usually up with my brother, Mike, and me in the mornings. As usual, Dad was up with us one day, but something that morning was different. I knew that I was the apple of my dad's eye, but he was introverted and not overly affectionate, which is why I was over the moon when he called me back up the steps of our large front porch as I was leaving for school to give me a big hug and tell me how much he loved me.

When I got home from school, Dad was in bed, which was unusual. I thought I smelled alcohol when I went into my parents' room, so I figured that Dad must be drunk. I had no idea where my mom and brother were that day. It honestly did not occur to my ten-year-old self that something was wrong, although I tried to wake my dad a few times. When my mom got home, it was dark outside. I exclaimed that Dad would not wake up. The next thing I knew, an ambulance was there with EMTs carting my dad out. What I did not know as I stood on the porch of my house that awful evening, feeling alone, scared, and shattered, was that my father had taken an overdose of pills as a means to end his life. It was not until a few days later that my mother told me what Dad had done.

What does a ten-year-old experience when she realizes that the father who loved her so much in the morning was trying to leave for good that afternoon? How do you make sense of a senseless situation? The answer is, I do not know. I did not know then, and I still struggle to understand it now. What I do know is that my little-girl self had disassociated—a self-protective survival technique used to escape an unbearable trauma—and left my body as a means to care for myself and tolerate the overwhelm. A dissociative experience is not unusual in a traumatic situation, and through working with several great therapists and energy healers over the years, I have reclaimed my inner ten-year-old and now keep her close to me, especially when I am triggered or experiencing a traumatic event.

After that attempt, Dad spent time in a mental hospital. I started to become aware of the major issues in my family. And it was not just my parents. Mike was a handful, and he would continue to be until he passed in 1997 at the age of fifty-seven. My mother became fixated on Mike, who was in and out of trouble and was deemed "otherly gifted" by the infamous Menninger Clinic in Topeka after a mental health assessment. My parents were told that his processing speeds were so fast and his impulsivity so quick that he had a hard time managing his day-to-day behavior. My parents simply did not know what to do with my brother, who was troubled, picked on, bullied, and constantly in trouble.

My mom always seemed to be at the school to deal with something Mike had done. He took "girly magazines" to school to share with his friends and farted in the classroom, causing such a stink that the teacher sprayed him with Lysol. My belief today is that he was lactose intolerant, and no one knew that dairy products could cause gas. He always found a way to cause a fuss. He spent much of his time in the hallway or the principal's office. Later, he wrecked his motorcycle, stole prescription pills from my mom after her neck surgery, and created all-around havoc for us.

Neither of my parents drank a lot when I was young. Later, they drank socially. When I was in the second grade, we moved to a new neighborhood. We had a pool in our backyard, and party time began. The neighbors came over regularly to drink beer and socialize. My parents started throwing fun gatherings. They hosted weddings and had an annual Fourth of July event. One year, my dad and brother dug a hole in the backyard, put a pig on a spit, and roasted it. There were some really good times.

Yet, as time went on, my mom was often found at a local bar and Dad in his basement workshop with a beer. When I was in high school, my dad woke me up late one night to get my mom, who had been pulled over by the police for a DUI. I remember sitting in my dad's old blue van while he tiptoed through the neighborhood, trying to see what was going on, because he had been drinking too. At the time, I thought the situation was messed up. I had school the next day, and yet I stayed up all night bailing mom out of jail.

Between Mom's drinking, Dad's depression, and Mike's erratic behavior, my role in our dysfunctional family was to be the good girl. In studying family dynamics later in life, I realized that I had been the hero, rescuer, and mediator all rolled up into one. It was a long time before I could untangle our dynamics and learn who I was on my own, just Christy.

First Love, First Heartbreak

After Dad's second suicide attempt when I was in the seventh grade, I started to disconnect from my family, although I continued to live at my parents' home until I was nineteen. My life, like that of many teenagers, was focused on friends, boys, and fun activities that kept me out of the house as much as possible. I had lots of friends, and in my junior high yearbook, I was nominated the "friendliest girl" in my class and participated in the "sweetheart court." I loved being popular . . . until the mean girls decided to target me and spread rumors about how stuck up I was. It was devastating, and I remember crying on my mom's bed, telling her how hurt I was.

This was the beginning of learning how to put on my big girl panties and deal with the reality that not everyone would like me. Big lesson! One I am still learning today . . .

High school was different. I thought I wanted to be a cheerleader, a popular girl, but somewhere along the way, the tides turned. I started dating a guy who was a great athlete but also a partier. Does anyone remember the terms "jocks, freaks, and frocks"? Jocks were the athletes, freaks were the partiers, and frocks were both. He was a frock. He loved to smoke pot and drink. We used to have big parties after Friday night football games. He would quarterback like a stud, and then we would get wasted at someone's house.

We broke up my junior year, and he started dating the really popular girl in school. My bestie at the time was dating his friend, so, as young kids do, she shifted her allegiance to her boyfriend and the new girl in the group. It was a challenging time for me. However, it was also around this time that friends of mine started dating boys from another school across the state line in Missouri. One day, we skipped class and went to their high school, roaming the halls and waiting for the boys to get out of their classes. As we were going past one classroom, I looked inside, locked eyes with the most beautiful man I had ever seen, and instantly fell in love. The bell rang. He walked out of the classroom and straight up to me. I was wearing a brown cowboy hat, and he tipped it up, looked into my eyes, and said, "Who are you?" He was a senior but looked like an adult—Italian, with dark hair, light eyes, and a build like a linebacker.

I spent my senior year of high school running across the state line to be with him and his family. A traditional Italian family, they were lovely to me. I spent Sundays with them, having what they called *basta*, which was a day-long feast with so much food. My first Sunday, I could barely get over the shock. His aunts served a pasta meal, then a full fried chicken dinner for the entire family, which included my boyfriend, his three siblings, his parents, grandparents, aunts and uncles, and cousins. Every Sunday, there were at least twenty people at a relative's house for *basta*. I had never experienced anything like it.

Late in my senior year, his mom got very sick. She was in the hospital for weeks, and we spent much of our time in the waiting room with the family. She ultimately died and left all of us devastated. She was such a remarkable woman, beautiful, fun, and so loving to her family and me. It was a terrible loss for the whole family, especially her husband and four children, ages nineteen, fifteen, ten, and six. Being the caretaker that I was, I spent a lot of time with the younger kids, playing, talking, and trying to love them through such a heartbreaking loss. My boyfriend was equally shaken. His momma loved him so much, and he knew it! Losing her changed him. We did our best to regroup, but as time went on, things changed.

We were so deeply in love in the beginning. He was my first love, though he had had another girl prior to me. One night after his mom died, I got off work and went by his house. I knocked on the door. No one answered, even though I knew he was there, and I knew he was with someone. I knocked, I pounded, I was losing my mind in angst and anger.

Finally, I went to the back door and could see him with his best friend and his previous girlfriend. They could see me now as well. He had no choice but to open the door. As he did, I pushed past him and went up the stairs to his bedroom. What once had been a shrine to me with pictures and small gifts on his dresser was now empty. I was gone, erased. Beyond devastated, I went back down the stairs and out the door without a word. There was nothing to say. My heart was broken, and there was no repairing it. It was all too much for me. I do not know how it finally ended. I kind of remember him coming around, leaving notes on my car, but I was numb. He had hurt me, and something died in me that night. There was no making up, forgiving, or going back.

Finding My Independence

At that time, I was working in two restaurants, one near my boyfriend's house and one in an area called Westport in Missouri. One night after work, I went to a bar with some coworkers and ran into a group of guys I had seen around Westport. They were older and always fun and entertaining. That night I met a tall, good-looking, well-built guy, and we hit it off. I remember walking out of the bar and getting into his beautiful metallic blue Mercedes convertible and thinking, "Holy shit, who is this guy?"

He changed the trajectory of my life. A business owner, a fabulous soccer player, and a smart, motivated guy nine years my senior, he was about to teach me some of the greatest lessons of my life. Early in our relationship, he encouraged me to read a book called *Seeds of Greatness* by Denis Waitley.

In *Seeds of Greatness*, Waitley demonstrates how someone can nurture the greatness within themselves. He developed a system that allows people to accomplish in months what takes many psychologists years. Based on the ten attributes, or seeds, which can lead to a fulfilling life, Waitley empowers readers to combine positive attitudes with their natural abilities, choose goals and follow steps to attain them, understand and be understood by others, and more.

This was the first of many books and tools my boyfriend would offer to help me build my self-esteem and ultimate potential.

These were indeed the seeds that have ultimately blossomed in my life.

When I started dating my boyfriend, I was still living at home with my parents. My parents were always strict with me, so I was surprised when they did not object to me dating a man nine years my senior. One day I told them that I would not be coming home that night, as I was staying downtown at a hotel with him. Even though I had graduated and was technically an adult, it felt weird that they did not say anything—so weird, in fact, that I brought it up. The conversation went like this:

"Christy, how old are you?"

"Nineteen."

"How long have you been doing what you want to do?"

"For a while now."

"Right, so what would you expect us to say?"

They were right, and that conversation set me free. I no longer feared the wrath of my parents, my mom's control, or that I would hurt my dad.

I started living my life the way I wanted. The older boyfriend was super into soccer. He was friends with the president of the local team, which came with great benefits, including suite seat tickets. One night, I invited my dad to a game. We all had beers afterward, and it was snowing like crazy as we made our way home. I remember driving my old 1970 Plymouth Fury with my dad riding shotgun, when he told me to pull over. My dad, always my caregiver, got out of the car into the cold Kansas night and started wiping down the windshield and clearing off the car. That was my dad. Although he struggled with depression and perhaps other emotional and mental health issues, he always came through for me. He always came to get me when I was in need. Today, I am so grateful for that snowy night, as it would be the last time I got to share a bit of my adult life with him.

Dad died not long after that. And it was not to suicide. It was a massive heart attack. He was forty-seven years old and alone when it happened. To make extra money, Dad always worked a second job. Mom, too. As a side project, they cleaned a local spa. The day his heart gave out, Dad had gone to the spa on his own.

He was pulling up to the spa when it happened. It must have been sudden, as he did not even stop the car. The old blue van ran into the building, shattering the glass window.

I was at my boyfriend's house when I found out. Early one morning, we awoke to Mike pounding on the door. Before I could ask what was going on, Mike said, "Dad is gone. Get your stuff. We need to go to the hospital." I remember feeling shocked and shattered, just like I had on that day almost ten years before when I had stood on the porch of my house watching my father being carted away by EMTs.

A million little pieces of myself walked into the hospital to kiss my dad's forehead and hold his hand for the last time—cold, with grease under his nails. He was dead. My dear, sweet dad was gone.

I had always been my mother's mother, for the most part, and the days and weeks following Dad's death were no different. Although submerged in my own grief, I took over like I always had. It was what I did. I was a little adult at nineteen, once again acting as the hero, rescuer, mediator, and, above all, the good girl who always got things done.

Gotta Love Your Brother

While I was still a senior in high school, my brother, Mike, true to his wild self, enlisted in the military. It was a decision that shocked everyone—first, that the military deemed him mentally stable enough to enlist, and second, that he did it. He was sent to boot camp in Texas. As usual, Mike shot off his mouth, unable to control himself, and created enemies. He told me that one night some guys rolled him in his bedsheets and beat him. It was about this time that he decided he had had enough and went AWOL, leaving boot camp. He wandered into the hills behind the camp. I do not know how long he was gone, but the story goes that while he was in the mountains, he came across the remains of a dead body.

Mike always had heart—too much, sometimes. It did not surprise me that he decided to return to boot camp and report the body. It ended up being a big deal. The missing person was well known in the community, and finding the remains ultimately resolved what had been a long, unsolved case. Mike became somewhat of a local hero. As such, instead of being punished for going AWOL and court-martialed or dishonorably charged, he was released from his commitment to serve and returned home with honor.

Mike was a good-looking guy and never lacked for female attention. He was fun and funny, and the girls liked him. A girl he met in high school became obsessed with Mike and stalked him. When she and Mike eventually did get married, she already had three kids from two different dads. Ultimately, they got pregnant with her fourth child. By the time my niece was born, Mike and his wife were crazier than ever. Working the system, his wife weighed over 400 pounds and would sit on her ass in their living room drinking soda and booze all day, ordering the kids around.

I do not remember her ever working. Mike had odd jobs. He was talented, like my dad. He could fix anything and was very handy. He did his best to support the family, but he was not the most stable and would go on benders. How they made it for as long as they did, I do not know.

I think Mike was always trying to do the best he could with what he had—as all parents do—but anger, alcoholism, and consistently poor decisions made him and his wife ill-equipped to raise a child, let alone four. Then, there was domestic violence that went both ways. They would have the most wicked fights and would call me.

I consistently offered to take custody of my youngest niece, but that would not happen until years later.

When his wife got her fifth DUI, social services stepped in. The oldest child had been out of the house prior to the arrest, and the middle two were put into foster care. My young niece was left with Mike until he got in more trouble and went to jail again. My niece went to live with my mother, who was seventy. When Mike got out of jail, he went to live in Wichita with Mom, her second husband (who was still alive then), and my niece.

Saying Goodbye and Finding Peace

Codependency always ran rampant in my family, and it might have been at its worst in the four years before Mike passed. There was significant triangulation. The "dreaded drama triangle" is the relationship between three roles people tend to assume: victim, persecutor, and rescuer. First described in the late 1960s by Dr. Stephen Karpma, then later renamed by consultant, coach, and speaker David Emerald in his book *The Power of TED* (*The Empowerment Dynamic)*, each role calls upon different tactics to manage activated emotional states like fear and anxiety.[6] In my family, I often adopted the role of rescuer. Everyone would call me, venting and voicing concerns. Mike would call and complain about Mom and how she was treating my niece; Mom would call and complain about Mike and his lack of effort toward finding work. It seemed constant, and with every new scenario, I tried to be objective. I learned a lot about myself and my judgements of my family around this time. I will share more about this later.

My mom had married her second husband, who was ten years her senior. He was a wonderful man. I called him my angel because he took on much of what I would have been worrying about. There was a reprieve in my life when he was there. He took care of my mom, my brother, and my niece in his home. He allowed me to focus on my own child and family in those early years. I am sure he did not anticipate these complications when he married Mom. I loved this guy. He was diabetic and ultimately suffered from a heart condition that resulted in congestive heart failure. I was at the house the week before he died. Losing him was a game changer, and the stress of Mike not working and Mikayla being a teenager brought my mom even more stress.

Just a few years later, my brother Mike passed away.

Mike had contracted Hepatitis C. His liver was significantly compromised, and he was undergoing treatment. But he was still drinking and his health was declining. Mom called me one day, saying that she just could not do it anymore and asking for help. I immediately flew out.

When I first walked into his hospital room, I was shocked by Mike's appearance. He was a skeleton. We talked, and the subject of his death came up. I said, "Do you want to die?" He said, "No." I said, "Do you want to fight?" He said, "Yes," to which I responded, "Let's fight." He fought hard until he could fight no more. Only four days later, he was gone.

My brother was always such a challenge in my life, but spending those last few days with him was beautiful. I felt Divine presence all around, and being able to draw from Divine guidance to help my brother move to the other side was a powerful, touching experience. I stayed with him the whole time and helped him cross over. I hoped he was finally at peace.

Mike's body was cremated. There was no funeral, as was the way in my family. Still, I felt strongly that we should have some sort of ceremony or ritual, especially for the kids. The girls wanted to do a balloon release ceremony. They went out and bought a big bunch of balloons, then gathered everyone so we could send the balloons up into the sky, toward Heaven, in memory of Mike. Mine got stuck in a tree—this big, bright, blue, shiny helium balloon. Two weeks later, I was back in Denver walking our dog when I saw a big, bright, shiny, blue balloon bouncing along the street. This balloon, with a bit of remaining helium, floated up into a tree and got stuck for a moment or two before the wind took it up, carrying it off into the sky. I stood there a bit dazed before bursting into laughter.

The same day we released the balloons, another mysterious thing happened. I have always had a mystical relationship with hawks. I once participated in a shamanic journey, and the shaman said I had a hawk sitting on my shoulder. Afterward, I was walking around a reservoir in Denver, and a hawk flew by and landed on a pole. I walked closer until I stood by the pole, and the hawk and I stared into each other's eyes. It was an unbelievable, mesmerizing experience. Later that day, I looked up the symbolism of hawk medicine. It has a lot to do with vision, perspective, and decisive action. The hawk symbolizes keen insights and powerful expansion. It is a visionary animal. I felt like I was being called into greater clarity and larger action.

On the day we released the balloons for Mike in the backyard of my mom's house, we turned to go back inside and saw a dead hawk splayed out in the yard. It was a breathtaking moment. I was a little worried about what it meant, but when I looked up the meaning, death and lying face-down both symbolize release. In my interpretation, Mike was telling us that it was okay; we could let go. I will never forget how powerful that experience was.

That was not the only time Mike visited with a message for me. In life, Mike loved farts and gross things. Well, his sense of humor finds me even from the other side. When Mike was still in the hospital, I flew to Wichita to be with him. At the hospital, I stopped in a gift shop. Among the plush stuffed animals, I found a monkey with sky-blue eyes, just like my brother's. Physically, Mike was my complete opposite. He had white-blond hair, beautiful blue eyes, and fair skin. I, on the other hand, have brown hair, brown eyes, and olive-toned skin.

When I saw the monkey with his blue eyes, I thought it was a funny gift, so I bought it along with a balloon. When I arrived at the room, Mike was cranky, miserable, and very sick; and did not appreciate the monkey, even though it made me laugh. My brother could be a real cantankerous jerk, and he was no different at the end. In my ego, there I was giving my all to ease his final few days, and he snapped and groused. I even threw the monkey at him a few times when he was pissing me off.

After four days in the hospital with him—with the monkey as my diligent companion—Mike died. I was exhausted. It was finally time to go home, and I took the monkey with me, those bright blue eyes still strikingly like Mike's. In the Wichita airport, they have a *Wizard of Oz* gift shop (surprise, surprise). Ever the Kansas girl, I stopped in, looking for anything to add to my collection (I have quite a few ruby red slippers). Just then, I looked down at one of the displays and saw a container of "flying monkey poop."

I burst out laughing. Are you kidding me? The "poop" was chocolate chip cookies, and the offbeat humor was so my brother's. So, of course, I bought some and brought them home. And I know, deep in my bones, that I will never see that flying monkey poop in a store again. That was a onetime message from Mike to me, telling me that he was just fine, still laughing his ass off at the oddities of the world.

To make things even more interesting, I was at that same hospital just four years later. This time, Mom was dying. I was taking a break outside, lying in the grass and grounding into the Earth. Suddenly, a couple caught my eye. Just as I started to get up and go back inside, they walked right past me, and I saw that they had the exact same monkey I had bought for Mike all those years ago. What were the chances of that blue-eyed monkey showing up again as I helped my mom transition? I knew it was Mike telling me that he was there, that he was with me, as I said goodbye to our mom.

Bring It All Back to Vulnerability

We all have our stuff. Our family stuff. Our inside stuff. Our outside stuff. And the things-we-keep-hidden-until-we-explode kind of stuff. We have our triggers, wounds, hurts, griefs and times when we do not feel good enough, strong enough, smart enough, or pretty enough. We might think that we are broken or on the verge of breaking. Mainly, I think many of us feel alone. But we are not.

There is no way to talk about being vulnerable without being vulnerable. Although this chapter is specifically about vulnerability, my goal is to share myself authentically all the way through, which means airing out some of the dirty laundry. But really, the laundry is only dirty or shameful if we see it that way. When we rewrite the endings—when we decide that our vulnerability is actually what makes us strong and courageous—we can find a way forward no matter what happened in our past. The truth is, shitty things will not magically stop, no matter what spiritual realms you explore. The nature of life is unpredictable, and being a "good" person doesn't mean "bad" things will not happen to you. Our job is to determine how we want to move through our lives, *no matter* what we face. And for me, recognizing the importance of vulnerability is one of the strongest stances to take.

TEDx Feature: Nicole Dority, "The Destigmatization of Mania in a Manic Culture"

When Nikki Dority graciously took the 2020 TEDxCherry-CreekWomen stage to give her talk, "The Destigmatizion of Mania in a Manic Culture," it amazed me, and as a social worker and someone very aware of mental health issues, I knew the importance of her subject. The way she approached the conversation was so authentic. With her hands over her heart, she readily communicated that she was about to share a very vulnerable story and might lose herself for a moment in tears, but she promised that she would pull it back.

I met Nikki, a well-known physical therapist and entrepreneur in the area, years before through networking in our Denver community. However, I had heard about her and how accomplished and seriously badass she was (and is) years before we actually met. We finally met through the company Nikki co-founded called Nurture, a community-based, wellness focused on self-care for everyone, with over sixty vetted independent beauty, wellness, fitness, food service, and retail businesses under one roof. I liked Nikki immediately. There was something about her authenticity and her genuine realness that resonated with me. Having heard so much about her career in the military, her family, her advanced degrees, and her successes as an entrepreneur, I humbly remember thinking that if I saw myself as accomplished, this woman must be on success steroids.

About a year after I first met Nikki, I heard about a challenging experience she had faced. Nikki had suffered a manic psychotic break. She was diagnosed with bipolar one disorder, and she was talking openly about it. Our mutual friend, knowing that I was a co-curator for TEDxCherryCreekWomen, suggested that I reach out to Nikki and encourage her to apply.

It was 2020, during the height of the pandemic. For the first time, we were livestreaming the event. I remember watching, listening to, and feeling Nikki's words fill up the vacant space, thinking about how much courage and vulnerability it took to share her story, especially as such an accomplished woman. As a ranking officer in the military, Nikki had supervised hundreds, maybe thousands, of military men. To take to the TEDx stage and share so openly about her experience with bipolar and mania was the definition of courage and vulnerability. And she was doing it to be of service to other humans so that we would not feel so alone.

Nikki began her talk by disclosing the manic psychotic break that she experienced in Mexico and the details leading up to it. She recalled waking up in a hotel room not knowing where she was, why she was there, or why a dear friend was with her. She explained that the two months leading up to this trip had been ripe with trauma. Her mother had suffered a stroke. A dear friend's husband passed away. Her grandfather passed away. Her mother had a surgery that did not go well. And another dear friend passed away.

As she was "coming to" in Mexico, not remembering what had occurred over the last three days, Nikki's friend described it to her—that she had suffered a manic psychotic break from bipolar one disorder, a disorder that Nikki had never known she had. During her talk, Nikki shared some of the details of the episode, such as running away to take a nap on a paddleboard and buying dinner for an entire restaurant, something she learned about when she later found the receipt.

Nikki then went on to talk about the stigma around mental health in the United States. She said, "About a million people in the US suffer from bipolar disorder. For women, the rate of anxiety and depression is 4.3 percent, and again, that is *only* what is reported. And I estimate a lot of that has to do with the stigma that surrounds mental health and what people experience and that people just do not understand and are not educated. People who have migraines or strokes, that is accepted around the neurological state of the brain, but with mental health, it is just not yet understood."

She went on to say that our culture lives in a fight-or-flight situation, and everyone is running around like their heads are cut off. Nikki wanted more for women who are already doing so much, like cooking, cleaning, grocery shopping, taking care of children, and dropping them at various activities, all while working fifty hours plus. It is too much, she said. It is unsustainable, like mania. And the experience is not without consequences. People's cortisol levels increase, inflammatory diseases emerge, and autoimmune disorders appear. With their unsustainable lifestyles, people fall into depression or turn to alcohol, addiction, or anything to numb the experience of a brain and body that cannot keep up.

This kind of life, she said, is similar to what she experienced with bipolar—things swing from high to low. "Our culture," she said, "in some ways induces this stuff . . . Mania drove a majority of what happened in my life. I did not know until I was forty-four years old that I actually had bipolar, so I think a lot of people spend their life with some of these challenges and they never know they lived with or had that problem."

Nikki went on to share some of her personal and professional history, saying that the only way she felt like she could love herself or be lovable was through success. She shared that she did well in high school, although she did attempt suicide once, which was her way of trying to escape the dangerous space of her home. In college, she decided that she wanted to do it all and that she would never rely on anyone again, which prompted her to sign up for ROTC and carry twenty-two credit hours a semester. After graduation, she was commissioned into the US Army. She went because it was "responsible," and she "would not need anybody." She was a company commander of a 180-soldier unit and then an operations commander for all medical operations for the entire Fort Huachuca post. She said her achievements were representative of what she believed at the time—that being incredibly responsible and successful was what she was supposed to do to love herself and feel worthy of love.

After leaving the Army, Nikki immediately began working on her master's degree. After completing her master's, she earned her doctorate while working full time. She and her husband had children, and life went on, as it does. She shared that it was not until after having her second child that things began to go downhill. But she did not ask for help, even though she was working on two startups, working full time, and raising two kids, because she was *fine*. Her husband was traveling a lot at that time, but even still, she was *fine*.

Nikki's use of "fine" struck me and even made me smile a bit. I love acronyms and use them in my personal life and often in my work with clients. *Fine* is a great one because it aptly represents the experience that so many of us are having today. When we say—either to ourselves or others—that we are "fine," what we are almost always saying is that we are feeling "fucked up, insecure, neurotic, and emotional." I think that, much like Nikki, most women today have had their fair share of feeling "fine." I certainly know I have.

Nikki continued her story, explaining that, even while feeling "fine," she went on to found Nurture, a company that focused on self-care, with two other people—an obvious irony that was not lost on her.

Bringing it back to the present, Nikki once again exercised significant courage and vulnerability, noting that she was standing on the TEDx stage that day even after the significant psychotic break in Mexico and a more recent depressive episode. Even after the breaks and the suicide attempts, she was there to say that she could not and would not be standing in the TEDx red circle without the help and support of her husband, psychologist, and psychiatrist. She had finally asked for and allowed herself to receive help, and she was excited. She was excited about learning how to set and maintain boundaries—something that many of us who have lived in codependent situations inevitably struggle with. She was excited to let go of what was once an enormous desire to please people, a desire to be so productive that she got more knocked off her laundry list by 11 a.m. than most people do all day. She was excited about self-love, acknowledging that when she was "going–doing–succeeding" on repeat—working, running marathons, and doing everything else at a nonstop pace—she was not loving herself and was, essentially, running away.

As part of her healing and cultivation of self-love, Nikki's therapist suggested that she try to start loving herself like she loves her child. And to practice another important thing: self-care. Nikki talked about self-care as initially being hard to identify, as it is often looked down upon and considered shameful or selfish. As Nikki's therapist said to her, "If we do not focus on our wellness, we will have to focus on our illness."

I love that Nikki finished her TEDx Talk by speaking about self-care and unconditional love. She described the many ways that we can embed self-care into our lives, saying, "Self-care equals things that aren't productive"—walks in nature that feed the soul; pleasure that can come through a beautiful piece of music when you sit down and listen; books that sweep you away to a magical place outside your own head; and, my favorite, fun and laughter and joy. Things that we might have once thought to be a waste of time are a part of the human experience, and if we allow ourselves to tap into that richness, it can change our lives forever.

As Nikki finished her talk, I felt honored when I heard her mention my name and something I had shared with the 2020 TEDxCherryCreekWomen speakers and staff before we kicked off the event. Each year, before letting the audience into the theater, I invite our speakers to form a circle on stage around the red TEDx carpet. We hold hands and simulate one human heartbeat—I squeeze the woman's hand on my left, and she does it to the woman on her left, and so on, until the squeeze returns to me. Once we connect our hearts with each other as a group, we send the connection and love into the auditorium, then to everyone connected to the event, then into the larger community, and then on to the one human race, as we are all one. We are all connected.

I felt Nikki's closing words deep within my heart. Here is what she said:

> Love. If we can think, as Christy was saying earlier, that we are connected by our hearts, that is everything—to our planet, to one another. We share an experience. It does not mean that it has to be bipolar, depressive, manic, whatever it is. We have a shared experience as humanity, and it is important that we do not think about the fact that, oh, somebody has this label, or somebody has this label, or somebody is not good enough. We are all good enough as we are. I send love to you. You are not alone. You are in community all the time.

When someone shares themselves with vulnerability, as Nikki did, you receive those words differently. *You are not alone.* Whether you are struggling with mental illness, with a difficult family life or past, in your personal or professional life, in your marriage or relationships . . . no matter what, you are not alone.

The Practice: Emotional Energetic Repatterning (EER)

Emotional Energetic Repatterning (EER) is the practice of reclaiming lost or disassociated parts of ourselves through the somatic space in the body. If there are parts of yourself that you feel like you do not have complete access to—whether physical or emotional—EER helps reclaim them.

Earlier, I told the story of my dad's first attempt to end his life when I was ten. The events of that night left me so overwhelmed that I disassociated. For years, although I was able to talk about it with my family, friends, and therapists, I still got triggered. When I felt emotionally overwhelmed, I froze. I was not able to stay present. When I finally started my own energetic healing, I was able to identify in my body where my ten-year-old self was located. Through the help of my coach, I would use EER to go in through my solar plexus, using my awareness, see myself at ten years old on the porch of my house, and enter the scene as my adult self to soothe her. This exercise unified that fractured younger version of myself, ultimately making us one again in the space of my body.

Emotional Energetic Repatterning is about reclaiming and repatterning parts of ourselves that we do not have full access to. When I reclaimed my ten-year-old self, I was finally able to stay present when I was overwhelmed. I no longer retreated to the energy of my ten-year-old self, who felt stuck and helpless. I could finally integrate her emotions and manage my life as an adult, remaining centered no matter what triggers came my way.

EER is best done with the help of someone trained in somatic trauma therapy. Energy from trauma can become trapped in the body. It helps to have a professional guide us in our journey of releasing it or repatterning it so that we do not once again get lost in the trauma itself. To learn more, please talk with a trained therapist. Know that there are options for you, and that your vulnerability can become a doorway to empowerment and love.

Oh God of Second Chances, may I come to the edge of my vulnerability and be willing to share my whole self, even if I am afraid.

4
_____

Why Have We Come to Earth?
(Remembering)

Why have you come to Earth?
Do you remember?
Why have you taken birth?
Why have you come?

To love, serve, and remember
Love, serve, and remember
—John Astin

I once heard a song in church called "Love, Serve, and Remember," originally by John Astin.[1] Along with the song's gentle melody, the lyrics offered a chance for deep reflection. I immediately loved it, so I added the song to a playlist on my iPod (back when those existed). One day, I was walking in a city park near my house. My feet gobbled up the familiar path, weaving through green spaces toward a lake. I was listening to Hemi-Sync, a company that aggregates music for synchronizing the two hemispheres in your brain.[2] As I breathed deeply, the centering music had me totally in the zone. As I rounded a corner in the park, starting toward a large Martin Luther King Jr. statue, my iPod abruptly stopped. I groaned as I started digging in my pocket, thinking I just needed to hit "play" again. I had been in the groove! Maybe it had run out of battery.

Then, out of nowhere, my iPod started playing "Love, Serve, and Remember." Chills erupted across my body—I can feel them now just thinking about it. Without explanation, I knew a message was being given to me. I always try to be aware of my surroundings, especially when something unusual happens that feels suspiciously like Spirit giving me a nudge. Looking up, I saw the Martin Luther King statue. With the song thrumming in my ear, I approached.

An incredible, towering monument, Dr. King stands atop a circular white stone as a tribute to his Nobel Peace Prize. Below, four others stand, metaphorically supporting him—Frederick Douglass, Mahatma Gandhi, Rosa Parks, and Sojourner Truth. Five people who gave their gifts to the world, who knew why they had come to this Earth. In their presence, with the song still playing in my ears, I asked myself the song's question: *Why have I come to this Earth?*

What happened next is still a beautiful mystery. Maybe it was because I had been synching the hemispheres of my brain; maybe it was the power of the people before me, their legacies and gifts still alive today; maybe it was Spirit helping me on my journey. Whatever the reason, I knew they were meant as my own calling.

To love, serve, and remember.

Even at the time, I knew I had been given an amazing gift. I had been given three purposes that would direct my life's path. It all begins with remembering who I am, over and over and over.

Remembering and Forgetting

It is not unusual for music to play an important part in my life. Have you ever heard the perfect song at the right time, and it lifted your spirit or helped you grieve? After hard breakups, I used to listen to "Here Come Those Tears Again" by Jackson Browne and "You Don't Treat Me No Good" by Sonia Dada. I loved when Sonia soulfully sang, "Lover, lover, you don't treat me good no more." Country music is my favorite, and I frequently tell the joke that goes, "What happens when you play country music backward? You get your lover back, your dog back, your car back . . ."

When my mom was in the hospital in her last days on Earth, I played the Anne Murray gospel album *What a Wonderful World.* "Lord, I Hope This Day Is Good," "Amazing Grace," and "The Old Rugged Cross" are just a few of the beautiful songs on the album. My mom loved it and told me once that listening to it brought her great peace. I am so grateful my mom made her peace with God in her later years.

When I was young, I would go to church by myself. My parents did not attend, but my best friend at the time went to a Baptist church every Sunday. The church bus would come by, and I would hop on to go to Sunday school. There were many things that drew me to church. It was a safe, comfortable, welcoming place. I made friends, and I loved the music. For a kid who felt like she could not control much in her home life, church was a kind of haven, and to be honest, it was also my social life. I thought it was a party every weekend!

> *Religion was not a passion I shared with my family. I remember coming home from church one Sunday after we had all been "saved." In the Baptist church, and perhaps other traditional faiths, there is something called*

an altar call, a practice that has become less popular in recent years. If you accepted Jesus as your Lord and Savior, you could be saved and guaranteed a spot in Heaven. For some reason—I was maybe ten or twelve—I stood up and went to the altar. I knelt down, the pastor prayed over me, and I was saved. It was a big deal.

But on the bus ride home, I started panicking. I may have been saved, but my family was not. The idea of them not joining me in Heaven was devastating. It felt like being abandoned all over again. While I was sobbing on my bed, stumbling through an explanation to my mom as to why I was crying, she said, "Oh, for God's sake, Christy. Don't be ridiculous!" My mom was not the most empathetic person. Although I can laugh about that moment now, I do not think she knew what to do with a little girl who was driven by a need for spirituality and a desire for her family to benefit from it too.

My relationship with churches evolved over time. Once, while still as a child, I went with a friend of my moms to a Catholic church. When communion began, I stood with the other churchgoers in my pew. This family friend put a hand on my shoulder and told me I had to remain in my seat. I could not receive communion because I was not Catholic. At the time, I was pissed, but maybe not for the reasons you would think. I just wanted to eat the damn crackers and drink the grape juice! Perhaps my religion at that time was not all about being saved so much as getting snacks *while* being saved.

When I was in my twenties, I found a Unity Church in Overland Park, Kansas. The pastor was hilarious, and the music team rocked. They even created their own album called *Remembering*. A specific song called "Remembering and Forgetting" jumped out at me even then. I still have a recording of it, and the lyrics are no less powerful now than they were when I first heard them:

Sometimes I feel the spirit,
Sometimes I feel so sad,
Sometimes I feel so near it,
Other times I hurt so bad.
Some days it all feels wonderful,
And some nights I want to cry.
Sometimes I feel like my dreams can become real,
Sometimes I just want to let them die.

Remembering and forgetting,
That is the game that we play.
We drift so far, we forget who we really are,
Till we remember that love is the way
To remember.

These words are so true. We often forget who we are or why we are here on this Earth. We get lost in our small dramas, or our big traumas; we numb ourselves with addictive behaviors or the need to keep up with the Joneses. It takes courage and stillness to remember who we *really* are: that we are pure Spirit, pure light, destined for greatness. Suddenly, in a moment of clarity, we remember. Maybe it is an iPod playing an unexpected song while near a monument to world-changers, or maybe it is the moment when our child shines their penetrating gaze on us and we realize that we are so much more than the stories we tell ourselves or those that society tells us. With clarity in our hearts, we remember, and we feel, deep in our bones, that we belong to something bigger than the limiting beliefs we have about our identity.

And then shit hits the fan, and we forget again.

The Hard Knocks of Earth School

This cycle of remembering who we are, then forgetting, then

remembering, then forgetting, is normal. I call it Earth School. It takes courage to come to Earth. Not every being gets the opportunity. I was born in a brand-new hospital in Overland Park, Kansas. I was the fourth baby born there. The story goes that, once I was placed in the incubator, the clamp on my umbilical cord came off and I started hemorrhaging. My mom later said, "Thank God the nurse found you that day." I thought to myself, I bet I popped that clamp off, thinking, "Hell no, I am *not* going. Take me back to where I came from!"

Life is no cakewalk. In Earth School, we have pain and hardship, wounds and scars. We get knocked down, people disappoint us, our needs are not met, and things do not live up to our expectations. These are all very earthly experiences. I think of it as being "down in the roots" of life. Based on what happens in our Earth School experiences, we develop reactive habits and behaviors to cope with the difficulties. This might include using people-pleasing behaviors to avoid rocking the boat. Or it could be developing a hard exterior to keep the pain out . . . and, consequently, the love, too.

Ascended beings (beings that are in the spiritual realm) do not experience the struggles of being human. But once we hit the density of the planet, we get this amnesia, and we forget who we are. But we do not have to see it all as bad—these experiences serve their own purpose. They provide opportunities for us to remember, ensuring we do not get so sucked into Earth School that we completely forget our deeper nature of Spirit and love. Remembering lifts us out of the roots of an unconscious life and back into the reaching branches of Spirit—aiming for the Heavens and soaking in the sun's rays.

I once heard a story of a little girl who was meeting her newborn sibling for the first time. The mom had returned from the hospital, and the girl was anxious. "Mom, I have to go talk to the baby!" The mom had no idea why, but she agreed, taking the girl's hand to lead her into the baby's nursery. "No," the girl proclaimed, "I want to go by myself." Still confused, the mom agreed. Watching from the door, she saw her daughter enter the nursery, lean over the crib, and say to the baby, "Please tell me where I came from. I am starting to forget."

When we are young, we still have an inkling of where we came from. This little girl knew that her baby sibling remembered, and she wanted a reminder.

I am not suggesting that Earth School is bad, or that we are supposed to remember our deeper nature all the time. Far from it. In fact, I believe we are sent to Earth School with one underlying purpose: to remember. And if we pay attention, Earth School gives us all sorts of opportunities to help us remember. Even the painful ones.

Forgetting Can Be Painful

Portia Nelson—American singer, songwriter, actress, and author—wrote a brilliant poem called "There's a Hole in My Sidewalk: Autobiography in Five Short Chapters."[3] It goes like this:

> *Chapter I*
> *I walk down the street.*
> *There is a deep hole in the sidewalk.*
> *I fall in.*
> *I am lost . . . I am helpless.*
> *It is not my fault.*
> *It takes forever to find my way out.*

> *Chapter II*
> *I walk down the same street.*
> *There is a deep hole in the sidewalk.*
> *I pretend I do not see it.*

I fall in again.
I cannot believe I am in the same place.
But it is not my fault.
It still takes a long time to get out.

Chapter III
I walk down the same street.
There is a deep hole in the sidewalk.
I see it is there.
I fall in . . . it is a habit . . . but,
my eyes are open.
I know where I am.
It is my fault.
I get out immediately.

Chapter IV
I walk down the same street.
There is a deep hole in the sidewalk.
I walk around it.

Chapter V
I walk down a different street.

It is amazing how many times we walk down that same street before choosing a different one—far more than four times, in my experience! My big joke is that we get forty to fifty years to figure it out—to remember who we really are—and then the Universe starts hitting us with cosmic two-by-fours. Some call it a midlife crisis. I see it as the Spirit saying that it is time for us to start remembering. We'd better start waking up, spiritually and developmentally, or the whacks are only going to become more frequent and more painful.

When I was in my late thirties, I started graduate school for social work while six months pregnant. I gave birth to my son, graduated, then went to work for a not-for-profit organization that supported women with low incomes who were transitioning into the workforce through supportive services, counseling, and group work. I ended up taking over for the founders and running the organization. With my son in preschool, I wanted to be a present mom, a good wife, and the leader of this important cause. Needless to say, I was burning the candle at both ends (if a candle had more ends than two, I assure you I would have been burning them too). One of my biggest challenges was that I tended to do more work for my clients than they were willing to do for themselves. It took going too far over the edge before I realized what a mistake it was to invest too much in other people without filling my own tank.

One day, a client came in at the very end of my workday. Charlie was in preschool, and my husband was working and always very busy. This client expressed that she no longer wanted to live and was asking for help. Handling suicidal ideation is a big piece of social work training. You want to be equipped to handle those possible life-and-death scenarios. When someone says, "I do not want to live anymore," social workers take it very seriously and go through a strict process that includes asking if the person has a plan to end their life and if they have resources to enact that plan, and, of course, intervening so the person cannot harm themselves. When this client told me she did not want to live anymore, I should have called 911 and got her to the hospital. Instead, I took on the responsibility of her care. She agreed to go with me to the hospital, and I drove her myself.

As I was driving, focused on my client, I remembered that Charlie needed to be picked up from preschool. I called my husband. He was not answering. There was a long wait for the emergency room, and I did not feel like I could leave my client alone. The tension of the moment escalated quickly—with a client in need of help, my child stuck at daycare with no one to get him, and my husband beyond reach, I started to panic.

The feeling was all-encompassing—like my entire body and thoughts were completely stripped from me. I could not breathe. I wanted to cry. I could not figure out what to do. You probably know how it feels when your amygdala—the part of the brain that controls emotional responses—gets hijacked and starts flooding your body with heart-pumping cortisol. Suddenly, your identity as someone who has everything "together" is being rocked, and you cannot figure out what you are supposed to do.

Finally, my husband called and agreed to get Charlie. My release was immediate and overwhelming. I was flooded with relief, almost shaking from the havoc that the acute stress had wreaked on my body and brain. Everything worked out, but it did not matter. By that point, I had already been so deeply triggered, it took a while to find my way back to normal.

That two-by-four had a big message for me: I had forgotten who I was and what I was here to do. I could not continue in that work position, taking on other people's responsibilities while raising a child. It was also the seed that led to an important motto in my social work and coaching practice: I will never do more work for a client than they will do for themselves. That cosmic two-by-four taught me that if I did not start with taking care of and serving myself first, I could not offer my gifts to the world.

After that, I left the not-for-profit world and used my privilege to become a stay-at-home mom. The Universe soon made it clear that there was another plan for me. Clients wanted to work with me, and I started a small coaching practice out of my home. Those circumstances eventually led me to start my now-thriving coaching practice and create an online curriculum to help leaders, creatives, and community members heal so that they can fully offer their talents to the world. The entire turning point happened because I faced that cosmic two-by-four—I could not ignore the pain in my life anymore. I had to remember who I was, what I was here for, and take the frightening steps to ensure that I listened to that message. Because if there is one thing worse than a cosmic two-by-four, it is the second one that strikes because you did not learn from the first.

Be of This Earth *and* Beyond It

I am not suggesting that we all ascend to become luminous beings who are not bothered by anything going on in the human realm. That is not realistic, and it is not what we are here to do. It is not about an "either/or" paradigm, but a "both/and."

On Earth, we are given free choice, and there are all sorts of tantalizing things around us—booze, sex, food, entertainment, material goods . . . all the indulgences a being could want. When enjoyed in a balanced way, these things add fun to our lives. But if we go too far, we get lost in gluttony, consuming more and more, yet unable to quench our thirst. Or, in another form, we become obsessed with our own reactive stories, believing the thoughts in our heads about how our life is supposed to go, or falling prey to what other people think. This reactive, self-indulgent way of living is called the "socialized self," and 80 percent of the world's population operates primarily through their socialized self. I once had a teacher who described the socialized self as our inner three-year-old. We are basically walking around like emotional toddlers who have not learned how to feel their feelings, succumbing to the whims of our reactionary emotions. We are driven by an external locus of control, thinking the answers are outside of us in the comforts of those earthly pleasures. We become enmeshed in Earth School.

On the other hand, if we reject all our earthly pleasures, we fall into the role of the ascetic, renouncing everything earthly in favor of a purely spiritual experience. Yes, we might not have the trappings of being human, but we also are not of this world anymore. We may even abuse ourselves for wanting decidedly human experiences, thinking they are beneath us or evil.

It cannot be either/or; we have to operate from a premise of both/and. We can enjoy earthly pleasures *and* find greater meaning beyond them. We can feel our grief fully *and* know there is a greater purpose. We can be fully human *and* fully Spirit. When we live in the world of both/and, we are not either the socialized self or the ascetic. We step into self-authoring, which means we write the stories of our lives by interpreting them through our higher selves. In leadership work, the "creative competencies" framework is all about responding to situations in our professional environments rather than reacting to them based on past conditioning.[4] From this place, we can design the life we want without pushing aspects of ourselves away. We are more whole and complete, and we can fully bring our gifts to the world in a meaningful capacity.

With our free will, we can remember who we really are. In doing so, we fully cherish and take care of the abundant opportunity that this life gives us.

At the end of the day, the choice is ours.

Forgetting Gives You a Chance to Remember

For any of you out there who might identify with perfectionist tendencies, I do not want you to get the idea that you are supposed to remember your higher self *all the time*. That is unrealistic. Forgetting is who we are. It is part of Earth School. We are conditioned to forget, to get lost in our daily lives, to think that a bigger house really is what we need to feel happy. The difference is whether we are working to remember who we are beyond these stories or if we are willfully giving in to the socialized self.

Many people live by the motto "ignorance is bliss." They think it is better to not know and avoid the work of digging beneath the surface of our reactive tendencies. The socialized self wants to avoid stress and discomfort at all costs, even if it means abandoning knowledge that could be useful in helping us reach freedom.

I first delved into personal growth work in my early twenties. When I came back from California after attending a three-day personal growth workshop with Barbara D'Angeles, I was as high on life. Feeling compelled to share my transformational experience, I headed into my suitemate's office on Monday morning. There, I plopped into the chair near her desk and proceeded to relive every detail from the weekend—telling her how incredible it was and suggesting that she might want to attend a future workshop. After a long pause, she said, "No, Christy, I do not want to do that work. I do not want to relive my past. I prefer to remain ignorant."

The saying "Ignorance is bliss" originates in Thomas Gray's poem "Ode on a Distant Prospect of Eton College" (1742). The quote goes like this: "Where ignorance is bliss, 'tis folly to be wise."[5] Face it: you were better off not knowing that, weren't you?

I get why some people would choose ignorance, but the truth is that when we turn away from our inner work, we choose to keep forgetting, and we will only ever get so far in our aspirations to feel whole, happy, and well.

Love, Serve, and Remember

When I received the message that I had come to this Earth to love, serve, and remember, I thought I knew what that meant. In a way, I did. But over the years, these three concepts have continued to open themselves to me in unique ways. Like a gentler form of those cosmic two-by-fours, the Universe continues to give me the lessons I need in order to understand my purpose.

Love felt like the easiest one. My mom said that I was incredibly loving as a kid. I would run up to strangers and wrap my arms around their legs, giving them a giant grin as I squeezed them in a hug. Then, as I got older, I conflated love with getting my needs met. There was a time in my life when I felt constantly taken advantage of, and I was always looking for external validation. I did not feel loved, and I felt underappreciated. But it is not like love was suddenly unavailable to me. We are conditioned to believe that getting our needs met is the same thing as love. We think that if someone meets our need that means love. That is not true. Love is love. Love is not being eternally nice and accommodating. That was my conditioning, my survival mechanisms. And if someone could not meet my needs, it was not a sign that they did not love me. It was just their own socialized self-responding revealing their limitations.

Like my little kid self-throwing her arms around a stranger's legs, love is overflowing, abundant, and compassionate. Love is everywhere all the time, and it is our choice to remember to tap into love whenever we want. We long to get back to that time as kids when our needs were met unconditionally (if that was the case for us). But that is not our journey now. As adults, we are here to remember (amazing how often that word comes up) that we already *are* love, and we do not need to do anything to earn it. It cannot be given or taken away. It is the essence of who we are.

There is a whole upcoming chapter about service, so I will not get into it too much here, but it is a huge part of my reason for being on this Earth. When I think back to those incredible heroes cast as statues in the park, I recognize that they were agents of service. They knew why they had come to this Earth, and they devoted themselves to their work. Rosa Parks used her body in protest and worked for racial equality, Gandhi fought for freedom through non-violence, Sojourner Truth was an abolitionist and fought to expand women's rights to include Black women, Frederick Douglass used his power of speech and writing to speak out against slavery, and Dr. Martin Luther King Jr. was the most visible spokesperson for the civil rights movement. Among many other accomplishments, this group of incredible people served fiercely. And their offerings made a difference in the world.

For me, service has been a way to heal through giving back. It helps me remember.

When the COVID-19 pandemic struck, I was walking my dog down the street and saw a food truck pulling up in front of a church. We were all struggling at that time in different ways. For some, the struggle was practical—*Will I be able to keep my job and afford rent? How will I school my children while working full time? Will my family members fall ill?* For others, existential worries reigned—*How do I make sense of this? How can I help when I barely understand what is going on?* Instead of succumbing to feelings of helplessness on that day, I approached the food truck. "Hi! Do you need any help?" I simply asked. It turned out they were a mobile food bank, and guess who started recruiting and running their volunteers after that chance encounter?

Serving them was an incredible experience. My son and his teenage friends even volunteered by running food from the truck to the cars as they pulled up. When I serve, I remember who I am and what this is all about: helping one another navigate this wild experience we call being human.

Remembering Takes Practice

As far as remembering goes, we have already covered a lot of ground. How do we remember who we are? For me, it's not just when I am serving others. I also remember who I am when I am in nature. I love being in nature. Just this morning I was walking my dog (a part of my day when a lot of magical things tend to happen in my life), and a leaf in the shape of a heart fell in my path. I just love the Universe. That tiny symbol felt like a reminder: *You are love, Christy. You are here for a reason.*

It takes practice to remember. It might happen in nature or around animals or when we are creating art or playing with children. Just as our bodies get stronger by routinely going to the gym, our capacity to remember increases when we practice. Every moment, we are being shown that there is something more. It all comes back to how you are looking at your life and whether or not you've practiced seeing this deeper truth.

At a yoga retreat once, while in the tearoom by myself, I saw a moose and her two babies outside. I kept expecting someone to walk into the room and witness this magical moment with me, but they did not. Internally, I heard a voice saying that this "moose energy" was just for me and no one else, and I should let it in. Later, I looked up the symbolism of the moose. Baby moose are the only animals that come into the world with their eyes already open. The message could not have been clearer: *Pay attention, Christy! Keep your eyes open. Remember, remember, remember.*

TEDx Feature: Dafna Michaelson Jenet, "50 in 52 Journey"

This TEDx Talk is a bit different because it is about Dafna Michaelson Jenet, my friend and co-curator and founder of TEDx-CherryCreekWomen. I met Dafna in 2008. We were both selected to attend a year-long leadership program at the Denver Metro Chamber Leadership Foundation—called Leadership Denver—which "transforms actively engaged civic leaders into community champions through in-depth experiences with a close network of new personal and professional relationships to last a lifetime."[6]

Fifty emerging leaders in our community spent one day a month focusing on different areas of concern in our community. Dafna and I were two of three people in a group from the not-for-profit sector. The experience was empowering for all of us, but Dafna in particular used that moment to springboard into greater service. I have always loved one of Dafna's mottos, which is that she does not complain about a problem unless she is willing to pursue a solution (a theme you will see emerging again and again in her talk).

Dafna—the author of two books, a Colorado state legislator, and an all-around badass—centered her TEDx Talk on a journey she took to all fifty states with a goal of meeting community problem solvers. At the time, as a single mom of two kids—then seven and eight—she could only travel when her ex-husband had the kids. After dropping them off on a Wednesday, she would fly to a state, travel 800 miles, meet as many people as possible, get back to Denver by Friday afternoon, pick up the kids from school, have a weekend, then start all over again (remember when I said she is a badass?). Talk about being committed to remembering what is important and why you are here on this Earth!

Despite the wild logistics, the experience had an incredible impact on Dafna. She collected stories from about 500 people in all fifty states, ranging in age from fourteen to ninety-one, representing a wide array of religions, races, and socioeconomic backgrounds. These people were our country. They were us. But something also distinguished these interviewees. Although they were ordinary, they believed in their community. They believed that if they looked at the list of complaints in their community, picked one, and did not wait for someone else to solve it, they could make a difference. And make a difference they did.

One strong theme throughout the stories Dafna collected was that people felt inspired by their children, or they themselves were children. There was something about the next generation that was captivating, full of promise and potential. When Dafna finally finished her journey and talked with her fiancé—now husband—about this treasure trove of materials, they knew something was missing. Dafna's tales were full of inspiration, and she did not want to keep them to herself. But how could she use them to inspire action in others?

In a conversation with the teacher at her children's school, the Ricks Center For Gifted Children, Dafna felt something click, and she thought, "She is all excited about what I am doing, and we are thinking, do you know what? Building a building, building a community, it is the same sort of thing . . ." The teacher then asked Dafna: "Why don't you come in and share the materials you have with the class?"

Dafna thought it was a great idea. A lot of her stories were captured on video, so she stayed up all night with her fiancé editing the footage, wondering which pieces would be most moving for these third and fourth graders. Dafna and her fiancé wanted the kids to understand that they also had the capacity to be community problem solvers—it was not just something adults did. No small task!

Dafna recounted the experience as follows: "The day comes. I walk into the classroom, and I say to Ms. Gay, 'How long do I have?'" A question, Dafna admits, that would have been worth asking in advance. The teacher said she could have an hour and a half—a seemingly long time, especially with eight-year-olds and nine-year-olds—and yet, by the end of their time together, the kids had solved a major problem at their school.

After watching the inspiring video of community organizers, in proper committee fashion, one student volunteered to be the chair of their board. Dafna proceeded to distribute a pack of sticky notes and a pencil to each student. She said, "You have one minute to write down one idea per page of a solution or opportunity in your school. How can we make it better? What is a problem you would like to solve?" As she describes it, "That minute—all sixty seconds—was taken up by these kids dreaming up ideas because they were given permission."

When the time was up, she collected the sticky pads and furiously stuck the problems to the wall. A theme started to emerge. Although these kids hated the macaroni and cheese served in the lunchroom (a problem that would have to wait for another day), the biggest problem came from recess, from something called "the distress table."

The scary-sounding term was coined by the children to describe a table outside, where no one wanted to sit. "A table in between two brick walls where no sunlight comes in—cue the cloud, cue the rain; this is where you sit when you've been spurned, you've been wronged, nobody wants to play with you, and you are having an all-around, no good, very, very bad day."

Even the kids who had never personally experienced the distress table still understood that it was the biggest problem at recess. No one wanted to end up at the distress table, and they all knew that if that problem could be fixed, recess would be much more enjoyable. The first step was complete: the problem had been identified. And in true kid fashion, they came up with their own solution, which, surprisingly, took the form of an acronym: HRBBAR— "Help Ricks Be Better at Recess."

By the end of the exercise, the kids had identified a solution and what it included—things like respecting each other, lending a helping hand, and being kind to one another. The power of the exercise was striking to Dafna. "They were fully engaged because they were given the permission to both identify and solve a problem that affected them."

Six months later, Dafna was invited back to the school. Whenever there was an opportunity, the teacher had given the students time to further develop solutions for the distress table. The students ended up with three committees: the Reviving Respect committee, the Playground Rovers Friend-Finders committee, and the same group that came up with the "HRBBAR" acronym. They had renamed the distress table the "MHK table"—short for "Make Happy Kids." And it was not just talk. Through their actions, these kids changed the history of their school. They wrote for permission to paint the MHK table bright orange, they organized donations of toys and games and books that went to the table, and volunteers were elected to sit there and befriend other kids "so it is no longer a lonely, scary, awful place to be."

By serving her community, Dafna supported these kids in remembering what was important: showing each other respect, care, and love.

Dafna ended her powerful talk with these encouraging words: "Kids can solve the problems. You have access to the kids. All you need to do is talk to them, listen to them, elevate them up to the role. But in order to do that, you need to be a community problem solver yourself." She walked the audience through a series of questions that mirrored those she had asked the ordinary people she had met around the country who were doing extraordinary things: "True or false: I have a list of things in my community, however I define it, that I complain about. True or false: I am willing to take action on one of these things."

She went on to say, "This is what the people all around this country did. They looked at that list and they said, 'You know what? This one thing is something that I can solve.'" Even if you are not the ringleader who can solve a problem, you can be the organizer, bringing together those with skills or resources who can solve it. By the end of Dafna's talk, I felt convinced that it is not enough to just complain about problems in our community—we have to do something in order to truly be of service. We have to remember what is important to us beyond ourselves, then go out there and take action. When your compass is strong, you will never be led astray.

And, with an enthusiastic ending, Dafna quoted her own daughter, who, upon reflecting on her experience serving the community of her school, said, "Go out there and get 'em!"

Remembering Our Future

I want to take a moment to think about "remembering" through a different lens—remembering our past versus remembering our future.

As humans, we are conditioned by the things that we "know." For example, we are conditioned to remember the past because it is something we "know." It happened, we were there, and we probably have some kind of memory as proof. As such, the socialized self is likely to repeat past behaviors, keeping us stuck in reactivity. This is why it is so hard to change. Maybe you know someone for whom life never seems to go their way. Even when something good happens, they cannot let it in. *Just wait, things will be bad again soon enough*, they think. No matter the evidence their life presents, they are determined to feel like the victim. It is hard for them to change! Who we think we are is formed over years of proof thanks to the past—*This is who I am; this is how my life has always gone. Why would I expect things to be different?*

Remaining trapped in our past socialized is a great way to stay stuck in the same old patterns.

But what if there was a different resource at our disposal? I was once at a HeartMath seminar with Gregg Braden, a thought leader and scientist from Kansas who was teaching about a concept called fractal time.[7] Within his model, he posits that there is an intimate relationship between the past, present, and future. By understanding the past well enough, you can know when it will repeat itself based on the conditions that led to an event in the first place. For example, if you know of a certain trigger that caused you to feel a specific emotion in the past (like feeling anger when seeing a picture of your ex on Facebook), you can anticipate that reaction in the future. As he was speaking, an insight bloomed in my mind, like a flashlight being turned on. After his presentation, I went up to him and asked, "In fractal time, if we can acknowledge that time is the same as the past, present, and future, what if we could remember our future?"

The idea seemed intuitive to me, though hard to articulate. If our present reality was shaped by our past, what if there was a way our future impacted us, too? He was not so sure, though he thought "remembering our futures" would make a good title for a book. The idea has continued to grip me ever since. Our conditions arise from our past, but what if we could *remember* our future? And what if we did it from a place of what we desired, then conditioned ourselves to move toward that reality?

What if we shaped our lives by self-authoring our futures?

Self-Authoring Your Life

I know it seems like I am going out on a bit of a limb here, but the idea of shaping our lives to our desires is not new. The Bible has many passages about living into your desires. One of my favorites is "It is your Father's good pleasure to give you the Kingdom."[8] Or there is the miracle question any good social worker or therapist asks their clients: "If you woke tomorrow and, miraculously, there were no limitations and you had the perfect day, what would it look like?"

It is amazing how our desires shape our lives. Distinguished social psychologist Robert Rosenthal demonstrated the secret power of desire in what became known as the experimenter expectancy effect. Essentially, when a researcher goes into an experiment anticipating a certain result, they will unknowingly behave differently toward the participants.[9] This effect has been witnessed across many disciplines—teachers who expect certain students to perform well will consequently help them more, leaders' expectations of employee performance lead to promotions, and researchers who expect rats in experiments to do well inadvertently give those rats more attention.[10] In essence, when we expect a certain outcome, we behave in a manner that brings about that reality.

What if we did this with ourselves? What if, by remembering our future, we started behaving in a way that was likely to bring that future about? This level of self-authoring puts us in charge of where we want to go rather than relying on our past as a predictor of our future.

Many years ago, I was introduced and trained in a 360-degree feedback tool that shows us where we are in our reactive tendencies versus our creative leadership qualities. My test results said that I was highly reactive when it came to "complying" behavior, which means being a "good girl" (you will not be surprised to know that!).

I would stay under a group's radar, taking care of things behind the scenes, following rules, and keeping my opinions to myself in order to avoid conflict. But my team reflected back to me that this was not helpful. When I withheld my opinions or was not decisive, I was ripping them off. By holding myself back, I was not contributing.

This behavior was born from a past belief system that everyone was smarter than me and knew more than I did. It was then that I started realizing the disservice I was doing through my compliant behavior, not just to myself, but to the people around me. If I wanted to make a change, I needed to know where I was going—the outcome I wanted to accomplish. Instead of being wishy-washy with my participation in groups or my life in general (which came from my conditioning), I needed to start being decisive about what I wanted and how to achieve it. I started telling myself that when I am in a group situation—no matter what it is—I have something meaningful to contribute. Even if it makes me want to throw up, I have tasked myself with figuring out what that contribution is and offering it. This seemingly small step has had a huge impact on the direction of my life. My entire coaching business manifested because I felt like I had something to contribute to others, a belief I learned from my future self many years ago. If you tap into what you want your future to look like, you never know where your self-authored scripts of today will take you.

ASPIRE to Your Desire

When I work with my clients on remembering their future, I emphasize that it all comes back to your desire—that longing deep in your heart; what you want if you could have all of your needs met and dreams fulfilled. If you do not know where you want to go, it will be hard to get there.

An acronym to help you define and implement your desire is ASPIRE. It stands for

Awareness now
Spacious presence
Permission to pause
Intention/desire
Respond versus react
Experience/evaluate

When you become *aware* of this moment, giving yourself a sense of *spacious presence* and *permission to pause*, you can reflect on your *intention and desire*. From that spacious place, you *respond* to the world (hopefully as opposed to *reacting*). Then you can *experience* and *evaluate*: did you get what you wanted? Do you feel more open and alive or closed down and triggered? At any moment, we get to choose how we behave. When we ASPIRE to our desires, we remember our future . . . and boy, does it look bright.

If step one is to know your desire, step two is to move toward it through your heart.

Just like we explored in Chapter Two, the heart always knows what it wants. When I trained with HeartMath, I learned that the heart knows where it wants to go even before the mind. We are trained to trust our heads, but really, they are often full of steam and "great ideas" that were mostly born from past conditioning. Earlier this year, I went back and attended my high school's fortieth reunion. When I left, I felt so sad. Many of my classmates continued to embody the old ideologies, old thoughts, and old behaviors that had become their lives. Nothing had changed, because they hadn't.

The truth was, I could have been there too. Coming from a small town in Kansas, I was not destined to go to college, get a good job, or get my master's. I was not destined to carve my own path into wealth and fulfillment. In many ways, it is by the grace of God that I am not working at a bar just blocks away from my childhood home. If I had not listened to my heart along the way and changed my desires, remembering a future I had not even seen, I never would have made it out.

The heart has an intelligence all its own. It knows where it wants to go before you ask it. When you step into a place of creating your future, do so from the heart. The heart will know what you want most. And if you are ever in doubt, I have learned three great rules for turning down the volume in your mind and turning up the volume of your heart to know when an answer to something is *Hell yes!* and when it is *Um . . . no.*

Rule one: Something I picked up is "doubt" means "don't." If you are doubting something, do not do it. It could be that you doubt whether you want to take that job despite the good pay, or you doubt if you want to be a parent, but everyone around you is having kids. If you are doubting a life path, that is your heart speaking, and the message is loud and clear—*Do not do it!*

Rule two: "Maybe" means "no." I get it. "No" is hard to say, especially to people you will continue seeing. When another mom at your kid's school asks you to help make the costumes for the school play and you let out a really long "maybeeeee . . .", next time, save yourself and the other mother the trouble—exchange it for a "no." Be honest with yourself—you know when your answer is *yes.* If it is not clear, say, "I do not have clarity yet. Give me time, and I will get back to you."

And if you have a really hard time saying no, use a tool my

client recently taught me: say "no" with a "yes." When you cannot do something, you can say, "I am sorry, I cannot do that. But I can do___." Then, fill in what you are able to contribute. This way, you honor your heart's boundaries while also making yourself available in a way that feels good.

Rule three: Make a decision and call it good. Do you know how we usually say, "Make a good decision"? Well, how many hours have you spent fretting over what a "good" decision is? No one gives you a rubric—you could question what a "good" decision is until the cows come home. That is why we reverse it: be ready to make a decision *first*, then call it good. Set down all the fretting and second-guessing. Let your heart be decisive, then let it go.

Let the Universe Take You

You might be on board with remembering your future, but you are also probably wondering, *Christy, I get what you are saying, but how do I do it?* This, my friend, is where we step beyond our comfort zone. When it comes to remembering our future, you do not need to know "how" to do it. Your job is to dis-identify as the "doer" in your life. Get clear about what you desire and let the Universe take you. We cannot force our future; we can only connect deeply with our heart's desire, pay attention, and take action.

When I was in my mid-twenties, I was putting myself through school. I had quit my job and was living off my 401(k). From the outside, although I was independent, my life did not look exceptionally promising. One day, my girlfriend was over while I was paying the bills. Out of nowhere, I turned to her, a feeling of lightness in my chest, and said, "You know what? I am destined to be rich."

And do you know what? By most standards, I am rich now! I do not say that to brag but to show you how strong desire can be. Did I know how I was going to get rich? Nope! And when I wanted to be a professional speaker in my heart of hearts, did I ever think I would actually give a TEDx Talk? Hell no! I even said no the first time I was asked. But when I got quiet and listened to my heart, I knew the right direction. I could not have planned any of this even if I tried. All my roadmaps would have looked pretty on the outside, but they would have been horseshit—a human trying to control the Divine's work. Still, I will say it again: none of it happens if you do not first start with your desire.

And when life finally gives you what you desire, you have to say *yes*! A long time ago, I chose two guiding posts for my life, and I told myself I would always invest in them: education and travel. Learning and experiencing the world are two experiences no one can ever take from you. Even as a young adult, I knew they would be valuable. When I was at my job, burning the candle at both ends, a girlfriend called me up and said she was going to Europe with her partner for a wedding. "Why don't you meet us there," she proposed. "We are traveling around for two weeks."

I listened with my heart in my throat. More than anything, I wanted to go, but I had so much on my plate, and I could not imagine getting time away from work. Everything would crumble if I left! I told her I was sorry, but I would have to pass. After hanging up the phone, I was struck by a mini cosmic two-by-four. *Why not? Why can't I go? Travel is one of the things I value above all else!* With a quick slap to my forehead, I immediately called her back and said I was going. We traveled through Europe for two weeks and made some of my most cherished memories. That was my first time out of the country.

You do not know how the Universe is going to show up to support your desires, but when it does, make sure you are paying attention so that you can say yes. I am not talking about being irresponsible or making rash decisions that could negatively impact your life and well-being. I am talking about how you can ASPIRE to your desire and remember your future self so that you are not trapped by your past self, who is only going to give you what you already have.

Let's be honest—it is time; you are ready for something more.

TEDx Feature: Maggie Johnson, "Seventeen in Quarantine"

Maggie Johnson is one brave seventeen-year-old. The COVID-19 pandemic hit when she was a senior in high school, and one of the ways Maggie coped was to write poetry. She told me that one night she asked for her dad's help with something online, and he was surprised to learn that she was publishing her poetry on Amazon! When she was little, Maggie had told her mom that she wanted to do a TEDx Talk. Maggie is highly attuned to her future. Even as a teenager, she knows what she wants, she knows what she is capable of, and she is not afraid to put her desires out into the world. There is no better example of what it looks like remembering our future than seeing young people doing extraordinary things, as Maggie has done and continues to do.

In her last year of high school, Maggie was told that school would be closed for only two weeks. Of course, thanks to the onset of a global pandemic, things went differently than planned. In those two weeks, she realized that this virus—this microscopic thing no one could touch or see—was keeping her from her friends and family and everything she loved. In that loneliness, she wrote a poem about humanity. If the virus was taking us out, she wondered why humans were trying to do the same to each other. We are just people, she thought. We should be loving each other, not trying to hurt each other.

This poem, the first one she shared in her talk, is called "the world was never ours."

> *and in these times of uncertainty and scare we are re-*
> *minded of our own morality*
> *the world is reminded of the pain and suffering that*
> *comes with being a human being*
> *regardless of technology advances, wars, and seemingly*
> *perfect lives*
> *we are nothing but cells with a conscience*
> *if something so small can take out the globe*
> *why are we trying to do the same to each other?*

The next poem she shared was written on her balcony over-looking the city, on the last day of summer. She realized that she could ruminate about all the things that had not happened that summer—all of the moments she did not get to share with her friends, the parties they did not get to throw, and the trips she did not get to take. But she had to stop herself. It was not all bad. Some of the most amazing relationships in her life would not have formed without the pandemic. Despite the difficulty, she and her friends had made memories and found creative ways to connect. Even more importantly—without the pandemic, she would not have written and published her book.

Maggie exclaimed, "I feel like the second that we stop focusing on just the bad, and we stop spiraling down these holes, is when we start to see a little bit of hope, and we start to feel like there is a little bit of purpose behind what is going on." And though she could not say what that purpose was just yet, she trusted it was there.

With this spirit, the next poem she shared is called "some divine plan."

and maybe we were never meant to see
what could've been without the world ending
the way our lives would have progressed without our
newfound strength
the memories or creativity
the relationships we built and the ones we found do not
matter anymore
the shallow pools we were swimming in became deep
holes of prosperity we never knew we needed
so i do not think we were ever meant to see
what could have been because without the world ending
our lives would never have changed.

In July, Maggie posted her senior pictures on Instagram accompanied by a caption about her online senior year. Some boy in the grade below commented on the photo. "Maggie," he wrote, "people are dying." The implication shook Maggie, and she immediately felt awful. Was she allowed to be upset that she was logging into a Zoom call instead of walking into a classroom at a time when people were losing their jobs or dying? She wrestled with this question for a long time. After much thought, she realized that humans cannot control how they feel about things . . . we just *feel*. One person's feelings do not devalue another's. It was important to her to not shame her own experience but continue to embrace it. From my perspective, it was as if Future Maggie were reaching out to Past Maggie, imparting her wisdom about what was important and what would help her get through a life of endlessly sifting through other people's opinions.

But that was not the only criticism Maggie faced. After publishing her book of poetry, people close to her had a lot to say. They told her she could not publish a book about a global pandemic. To her, there was the beauty in it all. The pandemic was the biggest story she had ever been a part of, and there were seven billion sides to it. All she could do was claim her own version of it. At seventeen, she hoped that by sharing her feelings, she could help someone else find validity in their humanity.

These thoughts were the inspiration behind the third poem she shared, titled "will this ever end?"

> *remember when it was April 6th?*
> *April 20th?*
> *April 30th?*
> *next year for sure.*
> *September 8th?*
> *October 8th?*
> *hopefully next semester.*
> *please stop crying.*
>
> *what if my life was not made up of*
> *half experiences*
> *where when things get good*
> *they disappear*
> *into my own little figment.*
> *but relax people are dying.*
>
> *my eyes burn from the screens*
> *and my head hurts from the tears*
> *my lungs burn from the masks*
> *and my heart hurts from the memories*
> *please stop crying.*
>
> *the days seem to slip away*
> *into the same mundane routine*
> *eating lunch alone*
> *virtual classes with no learning*
> *constant sadness*
> *but relax people are dying.*

will this ever end? continued
it never is easy, I know that
but I thought the world
could give me a break
something that I once adored
has me completely burnt out
please stop crying.

why is this the way
my childhood has to end
I cannot be solitude
overthinking everything
feeling so beaten down
but relax people are dying.

For her last poem, Maggie sought inspiration beyond our planet. She always loved the comparison of people to stars—how they glow on their own and shine even brighter in a galaxy or constellation. She also loved that everyone has a story to tell. Still, it was hard for her to accept that she would never know all seven billion stories and that even of the fraction of people she would meet, she would not know them completely.

One night, while looking up at the stars and thinking of the people she knew, she concluded that the people in her life had to outweigh the experiences she would never have. They had to outweigh the places she would never go, the people she would never meet, and the stars she would never get to touch. As she reflected on her support system, this poem, "trip to the stars," became one of her favorites.

there are so many stars I'll never see
people I'll never meet
places I'll never go

but for the first time maybe ever
the people that filled my world
my tiny sweet little world
were the people that made life worth it
the places I'll never go
the people I'll never meet
the stars I'll never see
do not matter anymore
because the world is far too vast
far too big
and that is okay
I do not have to see the world
I do not have to touch the stars
because my world was what I needed
the universe picked me
to be the person that I am
and the stars are mine
I see them in the people I know
the people I love
the stars are mine.

What a gorgeous soul Maggie is to share her powerful insights with us all. In her, I hear a voice that speaks with wisdom beyond her seventeen years. Through the medium of poetry and reflection, Maggie taps into her future—even into humanity's future—and reports back on what she learns. She shows us that, no matter how grim the world gets, there is hope to be found, even if it is borrowed hope from our days ahead.

The Practice: Love, Serve, Remember

Spirit told me that I am here to love, serve, and remember. In a way, all of these qualities are essential for a fulfilled life. Try these exercises for cultivating each in your life, or choose your own, then assess how you feel. What does it feel like to bring more love into the world, to serve, to remember who you are? What activities make you feel more centered, braver, and more like yourself? Consider how you can incorporate these qualities more in your everyday life.

To love, I will

use words of affirmation and gratitude with my partner

do one random act of kindness

list five things I love about myself

send a text to three people expressing something I appreciate about them

To serve, I will

do something small for someone without expecting recognition (like holding open the door, washing the dishes, or cleaning the coffee pot in the break room)

find an organization I am passionate about and donate or volunteer

babysit a friend's child so they can have a night to themselves

bring a meal to someone in my community who is struggling

To remember, I will

meditate for ten minutes

pay attention to signs the Universe might be sending me today

go on a walk and connect with nature

create a playlist of music that connects with my soul, then sit quietly and listen

Oh God of Second Chances, I trust that my heart's desire guides me to my future, one where I choose to love, serve, and remember.

5

The Illusion of Perfection

"Imperfect" actually spells "I am perfect."
—Unknown

If you look for perfection, you will never be content.
—Leo Tolstoy, *Anna Karenina*

When I was first asked to do a TEDx Talk, I said no. Even though I dreamed of being a public speaker, I did not feel qualified. TEDx Talks are about "ideas worth spreading." Sure, I had multiple successful careers and had overcome hardships. But what idea did I have that was worth spreading?

My friend Dafna, who is now my co-curator of six years, was clever. When I got together with her and her husband, Michael, to start planning our first TEDx event, she asked me again to speak. The part of me that wanted to fly below the radar was quick to repeat my first answer: no. "Why don't you give a little free-form talk right now?" she said encouragingly. The invitation was so unassuming, so laid back, that I said yes. I was not committing to a TEDx Talk by just sharing some thoughts aloud, was I? Little did I know, this was how Dafna would coach all our future speakers, too: by inviting them to just start talking!

So, I stood up in Dafna and Michael's living room and spoke on a subject that came naturally to me. In fact, I was surprised by how well-formed my thoughts were and how they started rolling off the tip of my tongue like I indeed had an idea worth spreading. As I reflected on my life, a theme started to emerge. At that time, my life looked pretty perfect from the outside. I had a thriving career, an incredibly successful husband, a beautiful son, a supportive and inspiring community, and I was living a life full of privilege and blessings. People often commented on that facade: "Your life is so perfect, Christy." But they did not know what you have already learned from this book—I had endured years of trauma and had worked my ass off in a number of therapeutic and energetic modalities. I was *still* working on myself, my root behavioral patterns, and my insecurities.

When I was done, Dafna said, "That is your talk." And before I knew it, I stood on that stage in 2016, centered on a circular red carpet, and gave my talk: "The Illusion of Perfection."

Brené Brown has a lot to say about the illusion of perfection. "Perfectionism is a self-destructive and addictive belief system that fuels this primary thought: If I look perfect, and do everything perfectly, I can avoid or minimize the painful feelings of shame, judgment, and blame."[1] I can relate to that. Perfection is its own kind of defense mechanism, often born out of our childhood experiences. Maybe, we think to ourselves, if we are without flaws, we won't experience so much pain. But as we all know (yet struggle to believe), there is no such thing as "perfect." No matter how beautifully furnished your house is, how well-behaved your children are, or how perfectly suited your job is to your strengths, there is no such thing as perfection.

I am not going to lie—my TEDx Talk is not perfect. In fact, sometimes I wish I could take it down. I am still really critical of it . . . which is kind of the point. It is really hard for us to shake our ideas of perfection, which is also why I am writing this book. It is another chance for me to remind myself—and others—that life is not about being perfect. It is about finding ways to be *real* and *authentic*. In my experience, this is a much more fulfilling way to live than chasing the unicorn of perfection. No matter how "together" someone looks, we have all got our stuff beneath the surface, and we are all on a journey of uprooting it before it grows into something foul.

Making Stuff Up

Perfection is born out of an overidentification with the stories in our heads. Our ideas of "perfect" are just thoughts, and they are almost always untrue. I call it Making Stuff Up, or MSU for short. When my husband comes home from work at 6 p.m., tosses his bag on the counter, then walks upstairs without a word, that gives me a lot of ammunition for making stuff up.

He is mad at me; is it because I forgot to text him back about our dinner plans? Or is he not happy to see me because he does not love me anymore?

And on and on and *on*. This is not reality. This is our brain making stuff up. Because, in truth, *anything* could be going on. Maybe he had a bad day or saw an accident on the road that shook him up. Or maybe he really had to pee!

There was a TV show I watched as a kid called *Get Smart*. In one episode, an officer went up to an elderly woman's car and knocked on the window. She rolled it down, then hurriedly started talking about the events she had witnessed on the road. He stopped her and said, "Just the facts, ma'am. Just the facts." Someone used to tell me something similar. When I was a social worker serving as the new executive director of an organization, I was completely stressed out. If someone pissed me off, I'd go into the co-founder's office and blow up. Inevitably, she would say, "Christy, just tell me what happened." I was wasting my breath making stuff up, working myself into a fervor that was unproductive. When I stuck with just the facts, the situation would deescalate, and I could look at reality more objectively.

We all tell ourselves stories. Stories about who we think we are or should be, stories about how the world works, stories about other people. These stories are often the result of our early conditioning and how we were raised. The environments in which we grew up taught us how to behave and how life is supposed to be. *I am supposed to be a "good girl" if I want to get love. Life is hard, and I will never get ahead. I am not destined to have a lasting partnership, just like my divorced parents. If I could just get a nice car, I would be happy.*

Years ago, I participated in a leadership development program at the Center for Authentic Leadership in Atlanta. Our facilitator was a woman named Jan Smith. Four times a year, twenty to thirty of us would gather in a hotel near Buckhead and spend three days learning and growing and pushing the edges of our personal and professional development. Jan was always clear about what was real and true and what we made up about ourselves. One of the most powerful tools she offered was exploring our Default Identity versus our Generated Identity.

Our Default Identity comes from the stories we have come to believe about our lives. Our Generated Identity is what we *choose* to believe about our lives based on our real experiences. I am going to share my personal answers for my Default Identity and Generated Identity and my responses to the three layers of the exercise — beliefs about myself, beliefs about others, and beliefs about life. This is a great exercise to do for yourself, too, and it will help you distinguish your default mode from what you aspire to. In my Generated Identity, you will see that two metaphors emerged: puzzles and pathways. Puzzles because I love jigsaw puzzles, and pathways because I love hiking and approaching a blind bend around which I cannot see. More on that symbolism in the next chapter.

Here were my answers:

Default Identity about me: I am damaged goods, a misfit, and invisible.

Default Identity about others: Others will take advantage of me and attach, then go away.

Default Identity about life: Life is broken, and I need to fix it before it is too late; life is highly dangerous and unsafe.

Generated Identity about me: I am a courageous, intuitive, and fascinated inquirer; I have the opportunity to see my unique piece of the puzzle as a much-needed piece of the whole.

Generated Identity about others: Others are jagged-edged pieces of a puzzle and need the whole picture to come alive; I have the opportunity to connect pieces together into something bigger than any of us.

Generated Identity about life: Life is unpredictable; winding turns give me the opportunity to surrender to the unfolding pathway I cannot yet see.

I carry a three-by-five index card with these messages to remind me (remember!) of what is true thanks to my Generated Identity. When we operate from our Default Identity, most of the stories we tell are things we make up. They are not founded in universal truth, but rather in our limited perception. When we live in the land of MSU, we leave our present moment. We live in the delusion that something or someone "out there" will make us happy or fulfill our needs. But, in my experience, "He ain't coming." It is up to us to find and live our *own* stories, to be the author, the producer, and the actors in our own movies.

When I am working with someone who is stuck in their stories, I have them fill out my "MSU versus Facts" worksheet. You can create it for yourself, too. On a blank piece of paper, draw a vertical line down the center and create two columns. The left column is "Facts", and the right column is "MSU." Start with the facts: all the things that are tangible, real, and measurable. Things that were said, and who said them. What were the *actual* words in the email? Facts only! Then reflect on all the things you are making up about the situations or your reactions to the facts.

Facts	MSU Stories

The idea of "perfection" has been sold to us by other people, and when we buy into it, we surrender our agency over our own lives. Even the Wizard of Oz's perfection is just an illusion. He spins this idea that he is all-powerful by sitting in the Emerald city like a god and speaking with a booming, disembodied voice from a giant floating head. He is great, he is terrible, he is able to accomplish all feats . . . until Toto pulls back the curtain and reveals a small, imperfect man with a megaphone pulling on levers and cranks.

But just knowing that perfection is an illusion does not always make it go away. That is why, as with any illness, we need an antidote.

The Antidote to Perfection

In her book *The Gifts of Imperfection*, Brené Brown lays out the consequences of unexamined perfection. "Understanding the difference between healthy striving and perfectionism is critical to laying down the shield and picking up your life. Research shows that perfectionism hampers success. In fact, it is often the path to depression, anxiety, addiction, and life paralysis."[2] Although we think perfection will get us the things we long for—success, belonging, freedom from pain and suffering—it only exacerbates difficult experiences. Fortunately, the antidote to perfection is also the pathway to attaining what we wanted all along: self-compassion.

Practicing self-compassion is one of the most difficult things to do. We are not socialized to turn inwards when faced with difficulty and nurture ourselves. In the past, self-compassion might have even been met with disdain. Sometimes our society has twisted ideas about what makes someone's life "good"—ideas that include suffering or victimization, as if you could prove your worth by martyring yourself and rejecting the things that would actually bring healing and contentment. Let's be honest: no one wins when they purposefully turn their nose up at self-compassion because of outdated, misguided ideas.

But let's start even further back. When we talk about a concept like self-compassion, it can be hard to define. Although it seems ineffable, there are actual behaviors that indicate high versus low levels of self-compassion. If you are interested, Dr. Kristin Neff, an associate professor of educational psychology at the University of Texas at Austin, is one of the world's leading experts on self-compassion. Her work really changed my life when it came to understanding self-compassion. She has a free online quiz that will give you a self-compassion score. The types of questions she asks are things like "When I fail at something important to me, I become consumed by feelings of inadequacy" and "I try to be understanding and patient toward those aspects of my personality I do not like."[3] By taking this test, you can get a better understanding of how compassionate you are towards yourself, right now, and what that looks like in practice.

The truth is, we are not alone in dealing with the mess of life. We all experience it. Self-compassion includes the realization that we are not alone, and we all suffer. By recognizing that we are not alone, we can start to quell the shame we feel about our lack of perfection (or our belief that we are not perfect). When we do not meet our expectations, or our mom's expectations, or our boss's, how can we still hold ourselves in a place of high regard and respect? How can we create space for our imperfections and embrace them as a normal, shared part of life?

My friend and TEDx co-creator Dafna had a difficult experience recently. We provide surveys after each TEDx event and take people's feedback into consideration for the following year. After our most recent event, someone wrote a horrible review commenting on Dafna's weight, of all things. It was deeply upsetting, and she called me. "Those f—king a— —s," I said, wanting to come to my friend's rescue. It was so clear to me that the review had nothing to do with Dafna and everything to do with this person's twisted ideas of "perfect." And Dafna, like the beautiful woman she is, also realized that this was someone else's shit, and that she loved her body. She turned toward self-compassion and let someone else's idea of "perfect" completely deflate in her wake, waltzing back into her life with her bold personality, her love for her body, and her unmatched ability to rock a sparkling, gorgeous dress.

Sometimes we need help in order to return to self-compassion. Our friends can be there to remind us that we are worthy of love, and that "perfect" is a bullshit ideology invented by someone else that will only ever make us feel "less than." I may have been there to support Dafna that day, but she supported me in turn by demonstrating what it *really* means to love being in your own skin.

My husband often does that for me, too. I am blessed with a husband who recognizes my gifts and knows how to support me in getting out of a rut. When I have gone down a shitshow road, worrying about something in my personal life like feeling left out of a friend group, my husband always reminds me: "She is always like that; you know that, Christy. This is her story, not yours." His logical reasoning helps me cut through my emotions in that moment and come back to what is true—that MSU gets us into *all* kinds of trouble, and our only job is to come back to the present moment, the facts, and what we can do about it.

I love the subtitle for Brown's book *The Gifts of Imperfection*: "Let go of who you think you are supposed to be and embrace who you are." It is the "supposed to be" that creates a lot of our angst. Because maybe, all along, we are not *supposed to* be perfect. We are supposed to be our glorious, flawed, unique selves.

We Are Not Meant to Be Perfect

Rebecca Rosen is a renowned spiritual medium. She lives in Denver, and I have had the pleasure of working with her personally and in small groups. She once published a great piece after doing a small group reading. A few members of the group identified themselves as "perfectionists." Rebecca shared a message with them from the other side, reporting that "their loved ones came through with a consistent message: not everything is meant to be perfect. In fact, there is no such thing as perfection in the way we understand it. Life is messy and unpredictable, and it can be hard to see past this when we are stuck in our ego. When we look at the broader, spiritual perspective, we see the beauty and the gifts in the imperfections."[4]

This reminds me of another written piece about transforming our harmful relationships with ourselves, particularly as they relate to our imperfections. My badass cousin re-shared this post on Facebook, and it impacted me deeply. The post was vulnerable and authentic, which I found all the more poignant as it was being shared by a woman I knew to be incredibly grounded and strong. I wish I knew the original author of the writing so that I could give them credit. These were the words, slightly edited, accompanied by a picture of herself:

I have H A T E D this woman . . .

Actually, I have not loved her at all most of her life.

I have fed her lies and told her she was not good enough and have allowed others to tell her she is not good enough.

I have allowed her to be broken. I have allowed others to treat her disrespectfully. I have allowed her to run through brick walls and battle for others who won't even stand for her.

I could not stop others from abandoning her, but I have seen her stand up and be a light for the world and love others despite all that.

I have stood paralyzed by fear while she fought battles in her mind, heart, and soul.

This woman has screwed up many times as a partner, as a daughter, as a mother, and as a friend because she does not think she was worthy of self-love or the love of others.

She has a smart mouth, a stubborn streak, and she has secrets. She has scars because she has a history. She has so, so many scars . . .

Some people love this woman, some like her, and some do not care for her at all . . . but she is beginning to love herself.

She has done good in her life, she has done not so good in her life.

Every mistake, failure, trial, disappointment, success, joy, and achievement has made her into who she is today.

You can love her or not—but if she loves you, she will do it with her whole heart.

She is dramatic and sometimes she is scatter-brained. She will not pretend to be who she is not. She will make no apology for who she is. Never will she again.

This woman is a WARRIOR. She is LOVE. She is LIFE. She is TRANSFORMATION and GRACE and BRAVE.

She will never stop learning or moving forward . . . she is me.

How powerful is that?! I also shared this post and was amazed by how many women it resonated with. These bold words are a way of recognizing our imperfections, yet finding empowerment in them. The truth is, learning to love and accept ourselves just as we are is one of life's greatest challenges; at least, it has been for me.

On a recent coaching call, I discussed authenticity with a group of female executives—authenticity as it relates to speaking up and being ourselves, flaws and all, even if it is uncomfortable. One woman said she felt like authenticity gets easier as we get older. I believe this to be true.

What would it take for us to "get this," no matter our age? Tara Brach, meditation teacher and author of *Radical Acceptance: Embracing Your Life with the Heart of a Buddha*, says, "The way out of our cage begins with accepting absolutely everything we are feeling about ourselves and our lives, by embracing with wakefulness and care our moment-to-moment experience."[5] This is part of the foundation of self-compassion: staying in the present, understanding what we are feeling, and releasing it. The illusion of perfection is strong. It might come back again and again. But if we are aware, we can start to identify it and call it what it is: making stuff up. That is when we can put that shit where it belongs—the garbage—and move on with our day knowing we are perfectly imperfect, just as we are.

Do Not Put "Perfect" on Others

When I finished community college and started my undergraduate degree, I began driving to the University of Kansas (KU) to attend social work school. I met a young student who was also going to the university. During the school week, she drove to my house and I would drive both of us to campus in Lawrence, Kansas. On our drives, we got to know each other, and her life looked pretty perfect. She was dating a medical student. She was beautiful, and she had a promising career ahead of her. Then one day, as we were driving home after class, she started telling me about her family. Shit got real. Her dad had come out as gay and left the family; she had troubled foster brothers and sisters. I cannot remember all of the details, but I thought to myself, "Oh my God, I will never judge someone based on my first impression again." This "perfect" girl had her own shit to deal with below the surface. By making up a bunch of stories about her based on what I saw on the outside, I unknowingly projected unrealistic expectations on her that honestly were not fair.

Now, as someone who can sometimes appear to have it all together, I know how damaging this can feel. Like people do not think you could possibly have hardships, even if they cannot be seen from the outside. Just think about how many celebrities or public figures we have labeled as "perfect" who took their lives, seemingly out of the blue. Another Kansas girl comes to mind: Kate Spade. She had an incredible career as an entrepreneur and fashion designer, creating a leading luxury brand for women that epitomized class, elegance, and style. And yet, despite the accolades, mental illness lurked beneath the surface, undoubtedly creating unfathomable pain until one terrible day, she left this Earth. By thinking of someone as "perfect," we take away their right to be a full, well-rounded human being with their own stories, their own struggles, and their own insecurities.

When we put "perfect" on others, we also engage in another harmful behavior: comparison. In her *Psychology Today* article, "Is Comparison Really the Thief of Joy?", Amy Summerville, PhD, writes that "more than 10% of daily thoughts involve making a comparison of some kind."[6] When we put our ideas of "perfect" on someone else, we also inadvertently put ourselves down further through comparison.

Trust me, I know the seductive dance of comparison. It can even feel like an addiction. We become completely consumed with holding up measuring sticks to our lives, making ourselves feel as if we need constant improvement, new clothing, or home remodeling. Social media feeds this beast. With endless filtered images capturing the highlights of someone's life, it is easy to tell stories about how "perfect" they are, and how "imperfect" we are in comparison. Just like the title of my TEDx Talk highlights, it is all an illusion. And we get to decide whether we want to spend our life chasing fiction or embracing reality and finding our own kind of perfection in it.

You Are Perfect as You Are

At the end of my TEDx Talk, I shared an important message. If audiences were going to take anything away, I wanted it to be this: love yourself and all your faults and flaws. We are all imperfectly perfect. We are human beings. And even with our imperfections, I believe in the inherent good of all people. Brown talks about that. She once asked her husband if he thought people were doing the best that they could. And her husband—whose objectivity reminds me of my husband—said that it is a helpful thing to believe. And if it is a helpful thing to believe, then yes, he was going to move through this world assuming people were doing the best that they could.

People are doing the best they can, including you. Perfection may be an illusion, but choosing to do our best is not. It is an action, one we can boldly take in the world. And it is enough to do our best, just as *you* are enough, exactly as you are.

Although my TEDx Talk is about the illusion of perfection, I share a lot of the same information in this book, so I wanted to feature another speaker who graced our TEDxCherryCreek stage in 2019. Mary Jelkovsky brought up one of the most significant conversations related to the illusion of perfection—body image. Her authenticity and grace moved everyone in the audience that day to tears.

TEDx Feature: Mary Jelkovsky, "Our Bodies Are Not an Image"

"Four years ago, a cup of mocha changed my life." Mary—social media phenomenon, author, and speaker—started her talk by taking us back to when she was seventeen years old. She had just won a trophy at a major bikini fitness competition, one of the largest in the country. She showed a picture of herself at the competition, an event she had spent six months preparing for. She worked out every day, dieted intensely, and lived with the belief that if she focused on fitness, she could cure her body image struggles. In truth, her pursuits only made things worse.

While people around her were saying how great she looked—how fit, how dedicated—inside, Mary's mental health was falling apart. Every piece of food that entered her mouth that was not part of her diet caused distress and obsession, even if it was a mere handful of almonds.

Mary summarized that time in her life succinctly: "What nobody knew was that behind her perfect bikini body was a broken girl that was completely obsessed with her weight." But she knew she was not alone. Mary acknowledged that too many of us struggle with not liking how we look. Whether it is going to extremes, as she did, or nitpicking a few things—*a little tighter there, smoother there, thinner everywhere while keeping the curves (but only in the right spots)*—many of us struggle, to some extent, with body image issues.

A few months after that bikini competition, Mary received a mid-afternoon text from her mom. "Want to meet for coffee?" Mary replied with "Sure, I'll be there soon." While driving to meet her mother, another text arrived from her mother: "Sitting outside. I got you a mocha." Mary's emotions spiraled. *A mocha? How could she? The calories, the sugar, the diary—doesn't she know I am on a diet?!*

Fuming, Mary pulled up to the café. Her mother saw that she was crying, ran to her car, and tried to open the door, but Mary would not let her in.

"No, Mom," she said, "I cannot believe you would get me a freaking mocha." Mary drove away, and the shame for lashing out was instant.

As she was crying, Mary's phone pinged with another text from her mom. Behind her on the TEDx stage, for all to read: "I just want you to know that I love you very much. I am here for you anytime you need me." Her tears finally ceasing, Mary took a deep breath, relieved that her mother had already forgiven her. In that moment, she let herself feel her mother's love—the love of a beloved person when she could not love herself.

That moment offered another gift—in her poignant reflection, Mary realized that her body image had robbed her of many of life's beautiful experiences. Even that day was thrown into new relief: what should have been a lovely coffee date with one of her favorite people became a disaster because of her fears about food. Mary was too busy hating herself to realize what she was missing.

The same dynamic, Mary said, can find us in numerous situations: the pool party we do not go to because we are afraid of being in a swimsuit or the get-together where we worry about the calories in a cookie instead of connecting with friends and loved ones. When we are focused on the wrong things, we miss out on so much, big and small. For Mary, these were experiences "like baking cookies with my little sister. And I missed out on the big things, like my graduation parties where I was too scared of the calories in the cookies, so I did not go. And also, my grandfather's seventieth birthday party, where my grandma had cooked all this delicious food and I refused to have a single bite because I was on a diet."

Zooming back out, Mary asked everyone to consider the term "body image." It is something we say to describe how we feel about ourselves in our physical bodies. There has been a lot of focus on helping girls and women in particular to cultivate a positive body image. Although the focus on feeling good about ourselves through the "body positivity" movement is good, Mary wondered if this hyper-focus on our image was part of the problem. Maybe the attention we place on our bodies—both positive and negative—is part of what creates our insecurities, discomforts, and low confidence in the first place.

Our society is rife with images, especially when it comes to younger generations who encounter them on social media. They see their image reflected back not only in mirrors, but also online, often beside the picture-perfect images of others. Mary explained, "It is no wonder that 96 percent of women report feeling unhappy with their bodies or wanting to change something." What an astoundingly high number! And then, here is one of my favorite quotes from Mary's talk: "But our bodies are not an image. They are an experience, and they are a beautiful experience." The distinction is so important. Many people let their *image* ruin their life *experience*.

After getting her mom's text, Mary realized that her body image struggles had led to her missing out on life. So, she made a decision: she would heal her own body image struggle by living her life and not worrying about her image. She also made a commitment to help any woman she knew who hated herself to shift her focus and change her life.

Mary then offered an exercise that is scientifically proven to break negative thought patterns. Step one: pause and face what you are feeling. Many of us push our feelings away by staying busy or deflecting, but our relationship to ourselves cannot change unless we first pause what we are doing and become aware. Step two: breathe and focus your energy and attention on the area around your heart. This shifts your focus from the mind to the heart, where you can cultivate unconditional love for yourself. Step three: let yourself feel the love. The word "let" was intentional. Mary said that we must first give ourselves permission to feel our love. Outside the realm of "perfect," what is one thing you can appreciate about yourself or your body? Speak to yourself as your own mom or best friend would.

Pause. Breathe. Let yourself feel the love.

This practice is useful for any situation. Any day when you do not feel like your best self, or when something about your body is troubling you, or your self-worth is low—pause, breathe, and let yourself feel the love. "Because in doing so," Mary explained, "you will turn those lowest moments into your greatest strength. In fact, I was actually preparing for this exact talk at that same café, while happily sipping my mocha."

I feel Mary's happy tears at the end of her talk every time I watch it—the blissful, deeply humble sign of someone who let go of her ideas of perfection and embraced the pleasure of simply living her life.

The Practice: Self-Compassion

Mary's advice for feeling the love is so central to working with the illusion of perfection. Self-love and acceptance are the antidotes to our shame-based drive for perfection. In her 2013 TEDx Talk "The Space Between Self-Esteem and Self Compassion," Dr. Kristin Neff said, "Self-compassion is not a way of judging ourselves positively. Self-compassion is a way of relating to ourselves kindly, embracing ourselves as we are, flaws and all."[7]

Sometimes we mistakenly think self-compassion is something we are either born with or not. But the truth is, it is a tool we can learn to use through repeated practice, making it an option we can choose to pursue in our dark and difficult moments.

On her extensive website, Dr. Neff has a page with many tips and tools for developing self-compassion.[8] One of my favorite practices is the Self-Compassion Break, which I will summarize here from her website.[9] This is a great practice for dealing with everyday experiences that cause stress, anxiety, or pain or somehow knock you off your center. With three simple steps, you can bring yourself back into the vast space of compassion.

To start, think of a recent situation in your life that caused you stress in the past or is still causing you stress. As you reflect on it, see if you can feel that stress in your physical body. Where is it located? What is the sensation or the highest level of intensity?

Now, say to yourself: "This is a moment of suffering."

This first phrase brings awareness to how you are feeling and gives it a name. You can also say, "This hurts," "Ouch," or "This is stress."

Next, say to yourself: "Suffering is a part of life."

This second phrase illuminates that suffering is a normal human experience. You are not alone in your pain, and, in fact, you are actually connecting to one of the most fundamental, commonly shared experiences. You can also say, "Other people feel this way," "I am not alone," or "We all struggle in our lives."

Finally, put your hands over your heart. Feel the warmth of the contact and the gentle connection you are offering yourself. The third phrase is "May I be kind to myself."

If that wording does not feel right, ask yourself what would sound supportive in this scenario. How can you express kindness toward yourself in a way that will resonate?

These three aspects of self-compassion will serve to bring you back to the present moment, expand your awareness outside your personal pain, and gently invite you back into the warm embrace of self-compassion. Use it often and generously!

Oh God of Second Chances, I am whole and perfect and complete exactly as I am.

6

The Surrender

Something amazing happens when we surrender and just love. We melt into another world, a realm of power already within us.
—Marianne Williamson

So don't you sit upon the shoreline
And say you are satisfied
Choose to chance the rapids
And dare to dance the tide
Yes, I will sail my vessel
'Til the river runs dry
—Garth Brooks, "The River"

Rivers are powerful and deeply meaningful to me. I have always loved water, and something about being on a riverbank and watching the water flow brings me so much peace. Over the years, I have collected a lot of things related to rivers—songs, poems, images. I am even certified in a therapeutic tool based around the flow of a river and our life's journey.

Esther Hicks is an inspirational speaker and author who speaks through Abraham, or the representation of infinite intelligence and pure love. She often says, "Oars up, baby. The river knows where it is going; the river knows where it is going." Not only does the river know where it is going, but when it is left to follow its own direction, it can do powerful things. A river cut the Grand Canyon. A river smooths jagged rocks, rounds stones. A river has directionality, and though we cannot always see it, the currents tug the water ever onward toward its destination.

So many of us spend our lives trying to paddle upstream. We struggle against life, or we try to control the flow rather than letting go, surrendering to the river. Or we are flowing downriver, and something knocks into us, throwing us off course. Maybe a log floats downstream, or we hit a rock jutting out in the middle of the water. Next thing we know, we are clinging to the rock, hanging on for dear life, and we forget to let go. We forget that if we just surrender, the river will take us in the right direction again.

I have had many experiences where I have clung to a rock or fallen tree for too long, resisting the river's inherent, intelligent pull. There were relationships I stayed in too long; friendships that were not working, but I did not want to admit it; contributions I was making through work or volunteering that had stopped serving me, yet I refused to quit. We can even hold on to dreams or ideas for too long, afraid to let go and return to the unknown.

Whenever I finally notice that I am clinging to a rock, I eventually take a moment to look around and realize the river is rushing past. Then, I practice surrendering once more: *let go, let go, let go.*

Oars up, baby!

Trusting the River's Flow

Recently, I took a group of women on a retreat in Keystone, Colorado. The river became a perfect analogy for our time together. I played a song called "River God" by Nicole Nordeman about how a river flows over rocks and takes off the rough edges.[1]

Rolling River God
Little stones are smooth
Only once the water passes through
So I am a stone
Rough and grainy still
Trying to reconcile this river's chill

At some point, we all hope to experience ourselves as the water pouring over a rock, smoothing it. On Sunday morning, I brought the group to Snake River, a beautiful, energetic river surrounded by towering pines. "Your job," I told them, "is to find a place to sit by the river and be with the flow."

Watching these women embrace the river—which was roaring with high flow—was powerful. They each found their own place of solitude. Some sat on the bank; one woman sat on a rock in the middle of the river; one reclined on a rock like a lounge chair; and another leaned back until her hair was caught by the river, its watery fingers tugging it downstream. They took advantage of the landscape, reveling in the river's lessons. I walked along the path beside them, checking in and offering my silent support. Once our time was done, we gathered. Their silence was meditative, their energy completely in their bodies. I asked the group one simple question: "Does the river know where it is going?"

Their answer was unanimous: "Yes."

What if we trusted the path of our lives like a river flowing downstream? What if we surrendered, knowing we will always be guided where we need to go? All rivers lead to the ocean. They have a final destination and a path to get there. Just as we do.

Barriers to Surrendering

I know surrendering is harder than it sounds. Our brains often get in the way, creating barriers such as fear, overthinking, old belief systems, a desire for control, and a lack of faith. I imagine a lot of us can relate to these things. We can look at a river and see its direction, but so many things can take us out of the flow. We are afraid of failure, afraid that we are going in the wrong direction, afraid that we do not have what it takes. No wonder we struggle to let go!

We like to think we are in control of life—that we are the ones manipulating the river's flow—but it is such a joke. When has there ever been a time in your life when things went better in your relationships, career, parenting, or personal happiness because you tried to be *more* controlling? For me, that is usually when things blow up in my face—when I'm struck by those cosmic two-by-fours—and I am reminded that the only way forward is to let go.

This ties back to remembering and forgetting, and our propensity to engage in making stuff up. Research out of the University of Missouri explores spirituality and the brain. Historically, scientists hypothesized that there was a "God spot" in the brain—a specific area we could point to that explained our belief in a higher power.[2] However, that hypothesis has been debunked; there is no God spot. Spirituality arises from a complex activation of multiple areas of the brain. Interestingly, when we focus less on the self, activation in the right lobe of our brain decreases and our sense of spirituality increases. Orienting ourselves around others deepens our opportunity to feel connected to this life and to a higher being.

Dr. Andrew Newberg has done some similar work. In his book *How God Changes Your Brain: Breakthrough Findings from a Leading Neuroscientist*, Newberg reports that our brains actually cannot conceptualize concepts like God and death.[3] So what do we do? We make shit up. When faced with the mystery of the unknown, we come up with our own answers. We are constantly making up stories about what God is, what God can and cannot do, how God wants us to be in the world . . . and it is all because we are terrified of not knowing. Of not being in control. What if, instead of having to know, we surrendered to the unknown? What if we let go of our fear, focused more on others than ourselves, and let the river take over?

As they say, there are three areas of engagement in life: your stuff, other people's stuff, and God's stuff. Other people's stuff is definitely not our business . . . but we better remember to not mess with God's business! For many people, surrendering their need to know and control everything creates an enormous sense of relief. *It is okay; Spirit has my back.*

Choosing Curiosity

I get that surrendering is frightening. One of my favorite visuals to help my brain when it is trapped in fear is to imagine a bend in a forest path. I love when I am on a hike and there is a bend ahead. I cannot see around the corner; I have no idea what to expect. A sense of curiosity and excitement, even awe, bubbles up inside of me at the uncertainty. *What will I find?* It is like I am a kid again, giddy. With that sense of wonderment, fear dissolves, and it becomes a game. I say "Marco," life says "Polo," . . . and I follow.

Choosing to leave Kansas City was really hard for me. My family was there, along with my home, my friends, my job. I had developed an incredible life and lifestyle. My then-boyfriend and I had been dating for a year and a half, and I felt like I had everything. But Kansas was not necessarily his long-term plan. He was living in Aspen, Colorado, and he floated the idea of moving to Denver. We decided to give it a try. That was a really hard year for me. I had worked in sales in Kansas City but could not find a position in Denver. I did not have a job, and I had to start all over with my relationships. Every time I went back to visit Kansas City, I ended up crying as soon as we landed back in Denver. I felt like a huge tree whose root system had been completely dug up and plopped somewhere new. I was not grounded.

It took a while for things to change. When I look back now, I live a life beyond my wildest dreams. My husband and I have created an incredible life together through our travel, work in communities, philanthropy, parenting, and careers. I had no idea what our move would bring. It was not easy, but by sticking with the river's flow, my life in Denver has become even more amazing than I could have imagined. And I would not trade it for anything.

It takes courage. Surrendering is not for the faint of heart. You often do not know where you are going or what challenges you will meet along the way. But I want you to know: it is a choice. You can choose to trust your life, to not live in fear anymore. FEAR is also an acronym: False Evidence Appearing Real. I once listened to a talk from A Course in Miracles[4] about the choice between love and fear. In every moment of our lives, those are our only two options: you can choose fear, or you can choose love.

When the market crashed in 2008, all of our investments took a downturn. My husband is in real estate, and I had only recently convinced him to put some of our money in the stock market. Before that, he lived, breathed, and invested in the world of real estate. When the market crashed, I had a big Oh shit! moment. I was standing in the kitchen, and he came in. I could tell he was in a place of fear. "I am going to call the broker and sell our stocks," he declared. Summoning my courage, I looked at him and responded, "We have two choices here. We can be in fear of what is going to happen in the market, or we can be in love and trust that everything is happening for our good; everything will work out."

Now, I am not saying that we were in any way responsible for the market eventually turning around. But I knew that making a choice out of fear would not lead us where we wanted to go. Whether it is your finances, your place of work, where you live, or your relationships, you ultimately get to choose how you respond to each situation. But I would encourage you: do not make choices while you are clinging to the rock out of fear. Let go, return to love's flow, and see what happens.

What If Life Is Happening for Your Highest Good?

There is a great poem by Lauretta P Burns called "Broken Dreams."[5]

As children bring their broken toys
With tears for us to mend
I brought my broken dreams to God
Because He was my friend.

But then instead of leaving Him
In peace to work alone,
I hung around and tried to help
With ways that were my own.

At last I snatched them back and cried
"How could you be so slow?"
"My child," he said,
"What could I do? You never did let go."

That last line really hits me: *You never did let go.* That is what it all comes down to: letting go. How can God or Spirit help us if we do not? If we keep trying to control things? What if life is always showing up for us and our highest calling? What if all we want is already here, and we can have it if we are willing to surrender and trust?

You get to choose your perspective in life. As Tony Robbins often says, you can believe that life is happening to you or for you. Even when shit is happening, you can be curious about what is unfolding on your behalf. The gifts are often found only in hindsight. I was talking to a therapist in my late twenties, and she said something I had never heard before. She told me I was getting to an age where I could develop perspective on my life by looking back and seeing things the way I chose. When you are young, you have not lived enough or developed enough to hone this kind of perspective. She was showing me that hindsight is a powerful skill and tool to cultivate. I could look back and see only trauma, or I could see the many blessings that were there beside the trauma all along.

I recently did a talk at CampExperience, an incredible organization and event run by my friend Betsy Wiersma. I spoke about using hindsight to look back at the adversities of your life and discover that they are often the most pivotal moments. The moment when my dad tried to take his life was pivotal; my brother and my mom dying were pivotal; my breakdown with the suicidal client was pivotal. All those moments and more have led me to where I am today. I have found ways to integrate them and, in doing so, made my life better.

On the other hand, I could look back on those same experiences and see a victim. You might say to yourself, *How fucked up is this? Why did this happen to me?* Guess what? Your perspective successfully makes you a victim. But where are you going to go from there? How is that going to help you get what you want out of life?

We each get these choices. It is part of being in Earth School. And the truth is, perspective is often a combination of the two—something is fucked up *and* we can find a blessing in it. As Rumi says, the wound is also the place where the Light enters you.[6]

Surrendering Is Not Giving Up

There is an important distinction to make about surrendering, particularly when it comes to us people-pleasers: surrendering does not mean giving up or acquiescing. It can be easy to equate "surrender" with "the other person must always be right." No. Surrendering has backbone; it originates from a centered place in your being where you still know your boundaries and understand what you want. The difference is you do not let your desire for control take over to the point of making you miserable.

If there is one place where I have learned this distinction, it is my marriage. I have been married for twenty-two years—in the relationship for twenty-five—and there were many times when I wanted to be in control. Whether it came to parenting, how we spent our time, or how we spent our money, I wanted things to go my way. And when they do not go my way, I acquiesced, considering my husband wrong in my mind but silently accepting the situation. It was a victim mentality. *Fine, whatever, we will do it his way. See how well that works out.*

This is not surrender. This is the ego playing games, building up its sense of importance even in the act of making itself smaller. I did this for a long time. It was a hard, uncomfortable dynamic that I created for myself, and it was all built on judgment. I judged him as wrong and myself as right, then martyred myself in the situation.

As I have grown in my personal work and spirituality, and as my husband has stepped more fully into his being, we have dissolved this dynamic and built a new one. One day, after some kind of argument with him, I distinctly remember thinking to myself, *What if I dropped my judgment? What if there is nothing wrong here?* Instead of nitpicking all the things that I perceived as wrong, what if I looked at the blessings in my marriage? All the things we do together, all the things we have done. The human we have raised together.

Just changing my thought pattern in this way helps me let go and return to the river's flow. I can let go of the need to be in control all the time, the need to be right, because at the end of the day, most of the things we disagree on honestly do not matter to me. I do not *really* care what kind of car we get; I do not *really* care where we spend the holiday. So long as the big picture of our marriage is balanced and supportive, what I really care about is our heartfelt connection and growing toward our highest selves, together.

There is a quote that says, "Do you want to be right or loved?" They are not mutually exclusive things, and there are times when it is important to be heard and recognized. But how many stupid fights do we get into with our partners that honestly do not matter? We get hung up on the idea of getting them to admit they are wrong and we are right so our egos can do a little happy dance. But do you ever really feel that happy afterward, or do you always feel like you wasted time and energy that could have been spent building something together?

My husband has jokingly changed the quote, and whenever he says it, it makes me laugh, cutting through the tension of the moment and bringing us back to what really matters: "Most people say, 'Do you want to be right, or do you want to be loved?' Christy says, 'Do you want to be right, or do you want to be married?'"

Humor is another great way to let go of the rock and return to the river's flow, feeling lighter and freer than before.

Surrendering in Friendships

One of the hardest places for me to surrender throughout my life has been in relationships, whether with friends or romantic partners. My mom used to say, "Christy, you will be able to count your true friends on one hand." For many years, I did not know what she meant. I have always been social, my life revolving around relationships and friendships. But as I have gotten older and have made the mistake of holding onto too many friendships for too long, I am starting to understand what my mom meant—only a few relationships will last a lifetime.

It reminds me of a beautiful poem by an unknown author called "A Reason, Season, or Lifetime Friendship Poem."[7] It goes like this:

People come into your life for a reason, a season, or a lifetime.

When someone is in your life for a REASON, it is usually to meet a need you have expressed or just felt. They have come to assist you through a hard time, to provide you with guidance and support, to aid you physically, emotionally, or spiritually. Then, suddenly, the person disappears from your life. Your need has been met; their work is done.

Some people come into your life for a SEASON, because your turn has come to share or grow or give back. They bring you an experience of peace or make you laugh. They give you great joy. Believe it; it is real. But only for a season.

LIFETIME relationships teach you lifetime lessons— things you might build upon to have a solid emotional foundation. Your job is to accept the lesson, love the person, and put what you have learned to use in all your other relationships.

Think about the people in your life over the years. Whether they were there for a reason, a season, or a life-time, accept them and treasure them for however long they were meant to be part of your life.

And when they are gone, be thankful for the gifts you received from them when they were here—for a reason, a season, or a lifetime.

Some relationships have a natural end. They are not meant to be lifetime friendships, like the handful of friends my mom mentioned. I am going through this transition with a girlfriend right now, which is really sad. We were together for a reason, but not a lifetime. I have to accept that and let the river's flow carry us both where we are meant to go next.

Perceiving relationships through the lens of a reason, a season, and a lifetime gives me a feeling of grace. When I want to hold on to a relationship that is clearly over because it is hard to let go, I remind myself that just because something comes to an end doesn't make the time together any less precious or meaningful. Just as the poem encourages, we can have deep gratitude for the things this person gave us, then gently let go of the rock and let the river carry us onward.

Sometimes Surrender Means Jumping

We often think of surrender as a passive act. To let go of the branch or rock means to uncoil our clenched hands. But there is another way to surrender: jumping. Feeling your fear and doing it anyway.

There is an image hanging in my office of a woman leaping between two cliffs. The quote beneath it says, "Leap like a lunatic, over the chasm below, your true self awaits you, now you will know."

One of the biggest surrendering leaps I have taken is changing careers. I was twenty-eight and had ascended quickly in the world of sales. I had a six-figure income and lived a comfortable life that could easily have continued. But the Divine was calling me to do something different. I had a big heart and a desire to serve people more directly on their healing journeys. When I told my friends and family about my decision to leave my job and study social work, they thought it was ass-backward. It took a huge leap of faith to cross the chasm between job security and prestige to go home, work in a restaurant, and be a college student. If I had stayed in sales, my life would look completely different now. I cannot imagine I would have had the same impact and level of service that has brought me so much meaning and joy. If I had not listened to Spirit when I did, I have no doubt those cosmic two-by-fours would have come for me!

The COVID-19 pandemic was a unique global experience in many ways. Something I found very interesting was the sudden, widespread dissemination of those cosmic two-by-fours. I can think of many people in my personal and professional spheres who realized that their life actually was not working, and they needed to jump into surrender. We are all so busy; it is rare that we get a moment to pause and consider something different for ourselves, something better.

One of my clients founded and was running a successful production company, but during COVID-19, it became clear that something else was calling to her. I could intuitively sense it, too. She was experiencing challenges at work with a business partner and at home with her spouse. As a result, she was incredibly unhappy.

Finally, she knew it was time to let go and leap. I helped the business partnership dissolve, and she left her husband, bought an RV, and is now traveling the country and living her best life. She is incredible.

Another client had a nice corporate job, but was starting to hit the skids with her boss. She started waking up to the chasm between where she was and where she wanted to be. I coached her in her transition. Just the other day, I learned that she now has a consulting gig with flexible time and none of the pressure of a high-profile job, and she is blissed-out happy. I could give you six more stories about women who jumped . . . and women who did not and are worse off now than when the first cosmic two-by-four came.

Jumping is scary. We do not know what will happen. Will we be caught? Will we fall for a little while? Or will we finally sprout wings and take flight? When someone is having a hard time deciding whether they should leap, I ask the following question: "What would it cost you to stay?" Leaving my career to become a social worker moved me closer to my dreams, but it also saved me from a life of "What if?"

You can do this. You are strong enough. And whenever you need a higher power to support you as you contemplate your next move, say the Serenity Prayer:[8.]

> *God, grant me the serenity to accept the things I cannot*
> *change,*
> *Courage to change the things I can,*
> *And wisdom to know the difference.*

Sometimes we are given the choice to leap into surrender, and sometimes we have those experiences that call us to the edge, and we are pushed into surrender. As a social worker and coach, I have supported many clients through one of the hardest things to surrender to: loss. The losses we face in life can take many forms. Loss of identity, loss of children in miscarriage, and the loss of friends and family members. I have also personally navigated my own losses, finding the ways in which surrender can be a great ally.

When the TEDxCherryCreekWomen team received an application from Laura Thomas, we knew she had to be on the stage, sharing her ideas about grief and her creative ways of living and leaning into the loss of her brother.

TEDx Feature: Laura Thomas, "Navigating the World of Grief"

One of the scariest things to surrender to is grief. When we lose someone—or when we lose a dream or job or relationship—the last thing we want to do is embrace that new reality. And yet, we also cannot run away from our grief.

In her talk, Laura Thomas shared her own story of learning to surrender to grief. As an author, speaker, and performer, she even learned how to take a bold, courageous *leap* into grief in the form of a one-woman play that she performed for audiences around the country.

Laura started her talk with a vulnerable story. When she was twenty-two, she stood at a threshold, but it was not the one she wanted to be standing at. As a college senior, she wanted to feel like the world was at her feet. Instead, she stood outside a hospital room. Inside was her older brother, Scott, her only sibling and best friend. He was in a coma after a suicide attempt.

Beyond that physical threshold was an internal one—Laura did not know if she could cross into the reality before her. If she could become the sister who stood by Scott's bedside and held his hand.

Nine months after she entered Scott's hospital room, he was lost to suicide. Laura found herself thrown into a world of grief. A world she knew nothing about and felt ill-equipped to navigate. There were the anticipated experiences—sorrow, heartache, and a desperate wish for life to be different. Then there were other, harder-to-describe experiences, like feeling a greater capacity for love and a newfound gratitude for life. Grief made Laura feel more alive, and she did not know if that was okay. She did not know how to talk about grief or how to feel it, so she stuffed it down, and she made grief a problem to solve or something to get over.

Laura recognized that we all know grief: not only in the loss of a loved one, but when life does not go the way we want, or we lose a friendship or dream, or we realize how hard we can be on ourselves. We might experience grief because of an illness, injury, or injustice; or we might feel political grief, ecological grief, or social grief. She noted that there is even grief in losing this precious moment—in an instant, it is gone, never to be reclaimed. "In some ways, big and small," Laura said, "grief colors all of life. But we do not really have a way of talking about it or making grief a part of our collective experience."

On her own journey, after stuffing grief away, Laura felt fractured. She deemed part of herself acceptable and predictable; the other part was unacceptable because it was shaky and vulnerable and sometimes a little broken. Straddling worlds, she felt like she had become half a person.

Eventually, she did not want that life for herself anymore, and she knew her brother would not want it for her either. So, she decided to do something completely different: she surrendered to her grief in a big way.

Her brother, Scott, had trained in theater growing up, and Laura had followed in his footsteps. Taking inspiration from that connection, she dove headfirst into her vulnerability: she wrote, performed, and produced a one-woman play about her experience with grief. On stage, she brought her questions, curiosities, joys, and pains to each performance, then invited audiences to participate in a discussion afterward. In doing so, she wanted to create an experience where grief was normalized.

Those discussions had some amazing results. Laura reflected on how grief can often overwhelm one person, and it might be because we were not designed to grieve alone. In those discussions, however, no one's grief was too big for everyone to hold together. And even though everyone had their own life story and background, together, the group healed a little from their overwhelming losses.

Laura said that she wanted to share a piece of her performance with the TEDx audience. She turned around for a few moments, then turned back to face the audience, telling them that, near the end of her play, she would wait alone in a room for Skype to load on her computer. On that video call, her parents would tell her that Scott had died. While waiting, she noticed a mirror above the desk. Looking into it, she could see that everyone was there—her dad's eyes, her mom's nose, Scott's eyebrows, her own mouth. Her family lived on in her, and she lived on in them; in her pain, she knew that she was never really alone.

Taking a moment to end her performance before returning to her talk, Laura came back with some final thoughts. "I think," she said, "that this is one of the gifts of grief. That it can connect us. That I could see a sparkle in your eye as you talk about a loved one and it could remind me of what I feel for Scott. Or I could listen to your experiences of grief and some of your words might feel like they are pulled right out of my heart."

She recognized that grieving is not easy or comfortable and shared three things that helped on her own journey. The first was to allow your feelings to be there. "Grief is not a sign that you are broken. It is not a sign that something needs to be fixed or gotten over. It is a normal human experience. We grieve big because we love big, and we are equipped to feel both."

Her second recommendation was to be gentle with yourself. We can be so hard on ourselves, but grief does not respond to demands or timelines. Grief has its own meandering journey—like our winding river—and the best way to allow it to unfold is to be gentle.

Finally, she recommended finding someone you love and trust and asking them to just be with you. Not to fix anything or make you feel different or better, but just to sit with you and let you know that you are not alone.

Then Laura flipped the roles and gave advice on what to say when someone is grieving. "Those illusive 'right words,'" she said with a smile. Although she admitted that everyone is different, she provided three things you can say to someone caught in grief's grip. "You could say to them, 'I am so sorry for your loss, for your pain.' You could say, 'I see you, I hear you, and I choose you, just as you are.' You could say, 'I do not really know what to say right now, but I would like to be here with you while you are grieving. I would like to hold your hand as you cross that threshold. Because maybe what is on the other side is not so scary or uncomfortable, or even painful, if we go together.'"

Community is a fundamental part of surrendering: although we have to walk this journey of life ourselves, that doesn't mean we have to do it alone. We have companions in the river's flow. And when we see someone stuck on a rock or fallen tree—whether they are caught in grief or fear or heartache—we can coax them to let go and join us back in the river. We are all going toward that vast, glittering ocean of a fulfilled life anyway; we might as well go together.

The Practice: The Flowing River Meditation

At all my retreats, I take participants to the water—a river in the mountains or an ocean at sunset, whatever we are near. I ask them to sit by the water and watch the motion, the rhythm, the flow. When we return to our retreat space, my first questions are, "Does the river know where it is going? Can you control the ocean tide? Will the sun come up tomorrow?"

Even if you are not near water, you can create the same experience for yourself through meditation. This guided meditation is adapted from "A River Meditation for Letting Go" by Emma Wall of Ocean Flow Fitness.[9] It is a great practice for when you feel overly burdened by the stressors of life. By using the power of visualization, you will release unnecessary weight and discover the ways in which a natural element like water can support you.

To begin, find a comfortable position, either sitting upright or lying down. As you come into stillness, feel your breath moving in and out of your body, like a wave advancing and retreating.

Imagine you are walking toward a river. When you arrive at the river's bank, pause and look around. What kind of landscape surrounds this river? Are you in a forest or on a mountainside? Are you on a beach where the river flows to the ocean? Or maybe you are in a wide meadow?

Now, notice the river itself. What is it like? The width, the color, the speed. Are there rocks in the river, or low-hanging branches bouncing in the water?

What sounds do you hear? Does the river roar or chatter over small pebbles? Are there animals flitting about? What scents find their way to you?

Sit beside the river and dip your toes or hand in. What is the temperature of the water? How does it feel as it brushes against your skin? Is the sun equally warming your body?

Look around nearby and find a leaf. Pick it up and think about something that is causing you stress, anxiety, or worry. Imagine unburdening yourself of these feelings by putting them into the leaf. Feel yourself get lighter as you shift those thoughts and concerns to the leaf. Now, place the leaf on the surface of the water and watch the river carry it downstream, toward the horizon.

As you continue your meditation, if another worry pops into your mind, find another leaf, transfer the thought, and release the leaf to the wild.

When you are ready, slowly rise from the bank and start to walk away from the river, thanking it for its generous spirit and its willingness to hold your life with you and for you. With three long, deep breaths, bring your awareness back to your physical body. Feel the light spaciousness inside, as if the river swept away any accumulated heaviness and left you clean. Gently open your eyes and bring yourself back into your day.

Oh God of Second Chances, I surrender into the flow of my Divine path.

7

Three Clicks of the Ruby Red Cowboy Boots—Coming Home to Yourself

There is no place like home, there is no place like home, there is no place like home.
—Dorothy, *The Wizard of Oz*

"There Is No Place Like Home".

According to an old Hindu legend, there was once a time when all human beings were gods, but they so abused their divinity that Brahma, the chief god, decided to take it away from them and hide it where it could never be found.

Where to hide their divinity was the question. So Brahma called a council of the gods to help him decide. "Let's bury it deep in the earth," said the gods. But Brahma answered, "No, that will not do because humans will dig into the earth and find it." Then the gods said, "Let's sink it in the deepest ocean." But Brahma said, "No, not there, for they will learn to dive into the ocean and will

| 165 |

*find it." Then the gods said, "Let's take it to the top of
the highest mountain and hide it there." But once again
Brahma replied, "No, that will not do either, because
they will eventually climb every mountain and once
again take up their divinity." Then the gods gave up
and said, "We do not know where to hide it, because it
seems that there is no place on earth or in the sea that
human beings will not eventually reach."*

*Brahma thought for a long time and then said, "Here
is what we will do. We will hide their divinity deep in
the center of their own being, for humans will never
think to look for it there."*

*All the gods agreed that this was the perfect hiding
place, and the deed was done. And since that time, humans have been going up and down the earth, digging,
diving, climbing, and exploring—searching for something already within themselves.*

—Maria Connolly, "Old Hindu Legend, Author Unknown"[1]

I love this short story, and though it ruins a bit of the surprise
of this chapter, sometimes it is useful to know the punch line and
work backward.

Many of us want to feel at home in our lives. We want to belong,
to trust that we are here for a reason. We want to feel comfortable
in our own skin and happy with who we are. Sadly, most of us
go through our entire lives looking for home outside of ourselves.
Although we might not look on top of a mountain or at the bottom
of the sea, as the gods mused, we look in other places, including
our family of origin, our material possessions, our social standing,
our professional accolades, or our external beauty. Sadly, Brahma

in the story was right: we never think to look for our sense of home and belonging inside ourselves.

Throughout Dorothy's journey in Oz, she has one goal: she wants to get home. She believes home is Kansas and being with her Aunty Em. Although she was not entirely satisfied in Kansas (it was, after all, a sepia-toned life), she still feels an increasing desire to return home, even as the technicolor world called Oz dazzles her.

Along the way, she meets new friends, who are really personified parts of herself: her head, her heart, and her courage. Only when she accepts these parts and brings them along on her life's journey is the secret to her desire revealed: she had the power to go home all along—it was inside her. Clicking her heels three times, she repeats, "There is no place like home." She *does* end up back in Kansas, but life will never be the same because she has found home in herself through the acceptance of all that she is.

Dorothy's journey is not about returning home to Kansas. It is about returning home to herself.

When I gave my TEDx Talk, I wore these sparkly, gorgeous ruby red cowboy boots. Putting them on felt amazing. I walked on the stage onto that famous TEDx red dot and delivered my talk. At the end of my talk, I clicked my red ruby boots together and asked the audience, how do you want to be? What Is calling you home? Whether you want to wear ruby red slippers like Dorothy, or you are more of a ruby red cowboy boots girl like me, you have probably had your own struggles with feeling at home in your life. More times than not, we can pinpoint where our adventure took a wrong turn: when we started looking for home outside ourselves.

Were You Buried or Planted?

As children, the first place we look for a sense of home and belonging is in our family and place of origin. This has certainly been true for me. Both of my parents had challenging upbringings, and for many years, I thought their stories of struggle were also mine.

My father was born out of wedlock in Denver, Colorado. Upon his birth, his mother put him in an orphanage, where he lived for seven years. Although my father did not share much about his life as a child, the little I heard sounded terribly depressing. He was sometimes left in his crib, crying, with no one to care for him. It still makes me so sad to think of what he went through and the impact it had on him. How many kids could emerge from a similar experience unscathed?

Finally, on his seventh birthday, his mother called the orphanage and asked for my father to be sent to New Orleans. She had married and was ready to become a mother. With his lunch in a sack, my father was taken to the station and put on a train by himself from Colorado to Louisiana. I can only imagine how terrifying that experience must have been, venturing further than he ever had, all by himself. For the first time, he met his mother and stepfather. It was not an easy arrangement. His stepfather did not appreciate my dad's intrusion into their lives. Their relationship remained strained, and my father struggled to feel secure in his attachments.

While Dad was still young, the family moved to Concordia, Kansas, where he went to high school. During that time, four of his best friends were killed in a car accident. It was an enormous loss that he did not know how to process. After graduating from high school, he entered the Navy, serving for four years before moving to Wichita, where my mother grew up.

Mom's story is not much cheerier. Her father was an abusive alcoholic, and her mother was fresh off a farm in Iowa. From a young age, my mother became the de facto parent. The second of four siblings, she stepped up to fill in where her own parents dropped the ball. Her own mother did not drive, struggled to care for their family, and never worked. She was very naïve. When Mom was fourteen, her father was killed in a car accident in Nebraska. Because her mother did not drive, my mom had to drive the family to the hospital.

My mom was a scrappy girl. There was a story told at her memorial that summarizes her spirit. After her father died, her mother started dating. One guy was pretty unsavory, and my grandmother finally told him to get out and never come back. Of course, he did not listen. So, my mom went to the back of the house and retrieved the shotgun, then pointed it at him and told him to get the hell out of her house and leave her mother alone. A brave moment indeed, though it did not deter the man from ripping the gun out of her hands and beating the shit out of her. My mom's younger brother pulled the man off and cut his face with a bottle opener. Finally, the man left. In some ways, that story summarizes my mom's life—it was hard, and there was violence. Often, Mom's scrappiness was what helped her get through, even if it was a trait I struggled to embrace as her daughter.

My parents met in Wichita, Kansas, when they were still young. Mom was around eighteen, and Dad was recently out of the Navy at twenty-three. Not long after, they married and moved to Kansas City, where my dad started a job with a power company, and my mom worked at an Italian restaurant close to where we lived. My brother was born shortly after they married, and I followed eighteen months later.

When I coach my clients, there is a question I ask to help them reflect on their childhood: were you buried or planted? As children, some of us were stuffed into the ground and buried under heaps of soil. We were not cultivated, watered, or supported in our growth. This could look like someone who grew up in an abusive family, was neglected, or generally felt like their needs weren't met. In contrast, someone who was planted received attentive care and generally felt supported in who they were. They were nurtured, felt secure in their attachments, and deep down, they had a sense of home and safety inside themselves.

Our childhood and other significant events determine if we thrive as adults or just survive. Both of my parents had tough upbringings—they were buried—and for much of our family life, this led to a sense of just surviving. I think my dad was depressed since his childhood in the orphanage, and my mom was always getting herself into trouble, even until the end of her life. One of the most painful examples was when my first husband and I were going on our honeymoon, and I left our wedding money in our house. While we were gone, my mom took the money and gambled it away. When we came back and I found out, I was furious. Her response was: "What is the big deal? I will pay you back."

As a result, I also felt buried early on, like I was just getting by. You know some about my brother, Mike, and what a challenging child he was to raise. Frankly, I do not think my parents were equipped to meet the challenge. There was a lot of yelling and frustration. I learned that if I could just focus on pleasing everyone, I avoided the worst of the crossfire. I remained calm, taking care of everything and everybody. But of course, that was not a sustainable way for me to live. When we are pleasing and passive, we minimize ourselves for the world, taking care of others first and foremost.

After my dad's heart attack and death when I was nineteen, I stepped even further into the role of mothering my mother (as she had also done for her mother). His loss was unexpected and devastating. Mom knew I would take care of things, so I did. I went to the funeral home and arranged the logistics of his service; I called family members, managed the food they brought, and wrote thank-you cards to those who supported us. I was her emotional support. She knew I was capable, so I rose to the role.

It was then, as I reflected on my dad's passing and my unusual role in my family, that I started the long journey of figuring out what "home" really was.

Your Place of Origin Is Not Your Home

For most of my early life, I had a hard time separating myself from the craziness and dysfunction of my family. My parents' trauma became mine, and I identified with the chaos in my house. It was a reasonable assumption for me to make. I did not know any different. In my search for home, I was looking outside myself for the Wizard—the person who had the answers, who would make me feel worthy and like I belonged. The phrase "home is where the heart is" did not fully register. I still thought that it meant my family, not a space inside my chest where I could safely rest.

This way of thinking brought me a lot of pain. I did not yet know the Wizard was an illusion, and I felt restricted to my family's story. As a result, I resisted my life, telling myself, "I am *not* my mom's scrappiness, my dad's depression, or Mike's craziness!" I rejected those notions, and I harshly judged my family for their challenges. I saw them as messed up, broken, and wrong. Those were the last things I wanted to claim for myself.

The one saving grace I had was that I knew I was loved. As insane as my family was, they loved me, even if that love was sometimes confusing. When my dad said "I love you" before I went to school, then tried to take his life that afternoon, it was hard for a ten-year-old brain to process. There was love, but even that was complicated.

Family of Choice

One of my greatest blessings was that I was always surrounded by friends and neighbors who saw me, loved me, and encouraged me. When I began working at the ad agency at age eighteen, I reconnected with a friend from my childhood and a neighbor whose kids I used to babysit. They both had been working there for a while. My neighbor Betty and I worked together in account services. We were the internal contacts for the sales reps across the country.

Betty was hard not to love. She was unpretentious, loving, kind, and nonjudgmental, and she was just plain fun. We had a great bond, and she became a sister and mother to me. She supported me through my dad's death, Mom and Mike stuff, and my crazy relationships. Betty grew up in a small town outside Hutchinson, Kansas. She had an older sister, and they maintained friendships with their small-town friends well into adulthood.

Betty, I remember, once suggested that I go on a girls' trip with a group of ladies, and I said yes. These girls—whom I now call my Sage Moms, or the Caryville girls—were all nearly twenty years older than me. For forty years now, they have been a significant part of my life. We still travel together at least once a year and have such a wonderful time, playing cards, laughing, and delving deep into loving and supporting each other. They make up the family I have collected throughout my life, not as a way to reject my family of origin, but as a way to recognize that I have been raised by so many people. One of the greatest blessings in my life is that people have believed in me, taken me under their wing, and claimed me as their own. I could not be more grateful for the large, chosen family I have cultivated, as well as the mentors who have indelibly shaped me.

Finding Mentors

Betty's older sister, Karon, was an up-and-coming executive at BCBS, a health insurance company. She was beautiful and confident, and she intimidated me at first. On our first trip together, I was so nervous that I could not remember her name, so I called her "What-is-her-name?" She still does not let me live that down.

Karon became not only a dear friend, but as with these other women in my life, she became a mentor. Over the years, I watched her go to graduate school to get her MBA, climb the corporate ladder to senior leadership in her organization, and ultimately break the glass ceiling in her industry to become the first woman to chair the board of directors. She coached me, sponsored me in opportunities that helped me grow personally and professionally, and modeled so many things that I wanted to create in my life.

My experience with mentorship, and the important role it has played in my life, is multifaceted. When I was twenty-six and joined the Unity Church, I started to question my ideas of home. My mom mentioned that her friend went to this church, and I might like it. It was a small operation with only about twelve to fifteen people in attendance at a time. When I joined, they were interviewing ministers. Part of their interview process included a trial sermon. There was this woman, Mary Omwake, who won everyone over. She was funny, articulate, smart, and adorable. It was no surprise that she became the minister, and with her enthusiasm and energy, the church started to grow. Eventually, they moved to a bigger location.

My mom was still struggling to find her footing after my dad died, and she was spending a lot of time at the bars. She ended up in rehab. Mike was unpredictable, as always, and I was at my wits' end. Mary took me under her wing. I told her what was going on at home, and she helped me navigate it. One night, I reached out and said I needed help. She went with me to an Al-Anon meeting, which supports family members of alcoholics or people dealing with codependency challenges. Mary sat there the whole meeting, supporting me and giving me her time.

It was at this church that I started hearing the music about remembering and forgetting, and Mary's stories from the pulpit were deeply impactful. The first one I ever heard was about how Jesus drank wine, so why were we so judgmental of people who use alcohol? As a child of an alcoholic parent, this was a profound teaching. My judgments started to soften. With new input, my perspective regarding my family members—and their roles in my life—started to change.

Over time, I became more deeply involved in the church. I got certified in Unity Basics 1 and "Attitudinal Healing" from A Course of Miracles, then taught classes at the church. I dragged my girlfriends to 11 a.m. service on Sundays, sometimes still drunk from the partying we had done the night before. No matter what was happening in my life, I knew it was important to be there. That church was changing a lot of lives, mine included. A spiritual awakening was happening, ultimately creating the life I live today. It started with learning something important: my home was not found in a place or other people. It was in me.

Finding Your Home Starts with Acceptance

Finding home in yourself is a primary teaching of the Unity Church. Unity was founded in Kansas City in 1889 by Charles and Myrtle Fillmore. Deeply spiritual, Unity was born out of transcendentalism. Its most fundamental teaching is that everything is in you. The Bible serves as a text based on faith, but we are all responsible for stewarding our belonging from the inside. God is in us. Through prayer and meditation, I was starting to sense the truth in that teaching. Mary brought in brilliant thought leaders from around the country, including the author of the *Chicken Soup for the Soul* series, Jack Canfield, as well as Mark Hanson, Marianne Williamson, Jean Houston, and Wayne Dyer, to name a few. The more I was exposed to new ideas and inspirational speakers, the more I started to really *get* it.

My self-esteem was growing, but there was one thing standing in my way: I harbored a lot of judgment toward my family. I wanted to find home in myself, but when I looked there, I did not want to see any of them represented. There was a deeper piece I had not yet addressed—accepting my family and where I had come from.

Especially with my increasing success as an adult, I became more critical of my family and my upbringing. I mean, it is hard to convey how fucked up my family was. My mom could be loud and embarrassing. The first Thanksgiving I prepared for my family and then-boyfriend, now-husband, my mom went to the local bar to find Mike. She ended up bringing everyone from the bar back to my house. She said they did not have anywhere to go and told them to make themselves at home and enjoy the meal I had made. I was mortified! Or take my dad, whose two suicide attempts were deeply stigmatized. And Mike's struggles were so unusual and unfamiliar to everyone around us. I did not think I was perfect, but for many years, I did not want to be associated with them at all. In my mind's eye, I went to school, had a good job, and rubbed shoulders with powerful people. Surely, I was not like my Kansas upbringing!

Doing work around criticism and judgment is pretty interesting. At some point, we have to turn the mirror around and ask: what parts of myself am I resisting? If we did not care about someone, we would not spend the energy judging them. But once someone starts to threaten something inside of us that we do not like, we build walls and push them away. Our judgments often are not about the other person at all; they are really about *us*.

I could make it about my family all day long—I had a lot of data to back up my claims. Instead, I started asking what parts of me I was not willing to love and accept. Leon F. Seltzer, PhD, writes in *Psychology Today*, "We must ask ourselves what it is we do not accept about ourselves and, as agents of our own healing, bring compassion and understanding to each aspect of self-rejection or denial. By doing so, we can begin to dissolve exaggerated feelings of guilt and shame, based on standards that simply do not mirror what could realistically be expected of us at the time."[2]

The key to coming home to ourselves starts with developing awareness of the parts of ourselves that we do not yet accept. Over time, I realized I did not have to judge my family, and I did not have to resist those parts of myself. The truth is I *am* my mom's scrappiness, my dad's depression, my brother's unpredictable behavior . . . and I am so much more, too. It was not until I started integrating these pieces of me, while also giving myself the space to exist beyond them, that I truly started finding home in myself. That is when, like Dorothy, I found that home had been in me all along. It was up to me to choose a different path for my life than the one on which I was raised, without making my family out to be wrong or bad.

If we want to be whole, all the parts of us that we are currently judging or choosing to see as wrong need deep acceptance. It does not happen in a day or a week. Through diligent, disciplined practice, we start to turn the mirror around and see what needs embracing. I love the phrase "Everything's neutral 'til you judge it." If you want to be in a neutral state and stop feeling angst over who your family is, what they say, or what they do, you must stop judging and start embracing. We can be both our family *and* so much more.

From Embarrassment to Humor

You now know some of the crazy stories about my brother Mike. Growing up, I often felt embarrassed by how different he was. For example, he loved farts. One of his favorite pranks was to sit on me and fart. It made him laugh and laugh. He could really let them rip, and oh boy, did they stink. There was one car trip where our eyes started watering, and we gagged. I even threw up! It was truly terrible.

Even still, Mike taught me how to laugh. One thing about having a brother who causes all sorts of random trouble is you get used to unwanted attention, and you learn to laugh at yourself. When I married my husband, there was a clear distinction between his upbringing and mine. He grew up in Kansas City in a large Catholic family, one of seven children. He went to parochial school, attended college, and built a very successful career. He was living in Aspen, Colorado, when we started dating.

When we were married at the Lake of the Ozarks, my mom, grandmother, and Mike attended. Mike really loved me, and I could not help but include him in everything. Our ceremony took place in a Japanese garden, then we had our reception on a two-story party yacht in a cove with other boats tied together. The night wore on, and it was finally time to head back. As we approached the dock, the captain shared the safety instructions over the speakers. He told everyone to stay on the boat until we were safely at the dock. And I will be damned if I don't hear a mighty *splash*! Mike had jumped off the second story of the boat!

I was mortified, yet I could not help but laugh. It was not until a few days later that mom told me he had inhaled so much gasoline from the boat that he was sick for days. She thought it could have killed him. What was he doing? Even still, the memory makes me chuckle. Mike received so much harsh criticism in life. Who was I to judge how he struggled and what he did as a result?

There is another outrageous Mike story that makes a great "two truths and a lie." Have you ever played that game where you share two things from your life that are true and one that is a lie, and the group has to guess the lie? Well, you are going to learn my secret—I always say that my brother was on the Jerry Springer show . . . and it is one of my truths!

Mike and his wife, Rhonda, decided they wanted to be on the show. They went through the appropriate application steps, then were flown to Chicago the night before filming. They also brought a neighbor and invented a story—they decided Rhonda was having an affair with him and was not in love with Mike anymore. As is typical with that show—and my brother—all hell broke loose during the interview. There was yelling, screaming, and things being thrown. The segment ended with Mike dropping his pants and mooning the entire audience in the studio and everyone watching at home.

When I watched the recording, I was so embarrassed! Then I remembered: Mike danced to the beat of his own drum, and in a way, I have learned that from him. I honestly would not be the person I am today if Mike had not been my brother. Despite the hardships, when I remember all the good things that came from our shared childhood, it is much easier for me to accept his role as my brother and appreciate the love he gave me in his own unique way. We do not need to like what our family members do or the things they have done in order to embrace how they've helped shape the resilient, passionate people we are today . . . and how we have hopefully cultivated a good sense of humor, too!

Three Clicks of My Ruby Red Cowboy Boots

If you were wondering if I have completely come home to myself, the answer is I am a work in progress, just like you. My mom passed away a little over a year ago. Up until that time, I remained her dutiful daughter. She called, and I jumped.

She called when my brother got out of hand, and I would fly to the rescue. Just before he died, she called, and I spent four days helping him cross to the other side. At one point, my mom became the primary caretaker for my brother's kids. When that became too much, she would call and I would step in, like when I put my niece in a wilderness camp program to help shift her life in a beneficial direction. I even flew in to help my mom put her ill dog down. I constantly felt like I had to take care of her. As the dutiful daughter, I believed it was expected of me, and I always responded, trying to fix everything for her. To some extent, I felt like I could. As a successful adult, I had the means, and my social work training also put me in a unique position to help. But that does not mean the role was life-giving. Usually, it was the opposite. I felt like I was doing it for my mom's benefit—and because it was familiar to me and safe—not because it was who I wanted to be.

At one point, I learned something about my mom that helped me understand her better and realize why she leaned so heavily on me. About ten years ago, I was visiting after she had had a hip replacement. She pointed to a box of my dad's stuff that she wanted me to go through. Inside was a collection of articles about a horrible car wreck in which a man was killed just a few years before my dad died. I would have been a senior in high school. Mom was stoned enough on painkillers from her surgery that when I asked who the man was, she told me.

"He was the love of my life," she said. I was stunned. And yet, so many things started to fall into place. She had had an affair for fifteen years, starting when I was in kindergarten. The man was an affluent builder. Part of the chaos of my childhood stemmed from the fact that my mom would go out and party, doing whatever she wanted; now I knew she was doing it with this man. When he died, she had had a nervous breakdown. She was hospitalized, though it was called "alcohol treatment" at the time. Then, when Dad died just a few years later, it was a double whammy. She did not know how to function and leaned heavily on me. I did not have all the information at the time; I just took care of things and got shit done, making sure everyone else was okay. But now, in hindsight, I can see that she was devastated by a double loss and really did not have it in her to take care of things.

Still, it was not until a few months after my mom died that I could really separate myself from the role of the "dutiful daughter." I was walking my dog and listening to Glennon Doyle's incredibly powerful book, *Untamed*. Doyle, bestselling author and activist, was sharing a story of when she and her wife, Abby, married and were starting their life as a family in Florida. Her previous marriage to her husband had ended, and they were now co-parenting their three children. Her mother was not enthusiastic about her daughter's gay marriage, but she wanted to visit her grandchildren. Glennon took a stand, defending her own sense of home and belonging. She told her mother no—if you are not all-in on love island, you cannot come. If you cannot hold the space for what is perfect and loving, you cannot come. She said it was the hardest thing she had ever done, but that "A woman becomes a responsible parent when she stops being an obedient daughter."[3]

It reminded me of another story Mary shared from the pulpit of our Unity Church. I am not sure if this is true, but the image and message are remarkable, regardless. Years ago, there was a terrible fire in Yellowstone National Park. Mary read on the news that, as the firefighters were walking through the burned timbers, they found a dead eagle with her wings spread out on the ground, her whole back charred. When they turned her over, a group of chicks ran out. The fierce mother had lain over her babies during the fire so they could survive. Whether or not it was true, the image deeply impacted me. A story of a mother's love, of fierce priorities.

Glennon's response to her mother had the same fiery response, and it stopped me in my tracks on the sidewalk. Although I could not draw those boundaries with my mom anymore, I realized that I was no longer an obedient daughter. I could be fully who I was. At that moment, I came home to myself. I recognized that everything I was looking for was in me, as me. For most of my life, I had been wearing my superhero cape, helping others—through social work; with my mom, dad, brother, nieces, and nephews; and as a therapist. To set all that responsibility down and just be me was a huge relief.

My mom's passing opened a portal to help me realize that I had had this capacity in me the whole time. With three simple clicks of my ruby red cowboy boots, I was home. No matter if you are in a sepia-toned world or walking through the technicolor world of Oz trying to find home and not sure where to look, your journey will always lead you back to the same place: yourself. The place where all your quirks and histories and mistakes and triumphs reside. The place where you are everything that has ever impacted you, and also far more. The place where you can set down your judgments, accept yourself and your circumstances, and say to yourself, with quiet confidence in your heart, *there is no place like home.*

TEDx Feature: Betsy Wiersma, "Choose Your Family, Change Your Life".

Betsy Wiersma is a force to be reckoned with. A social entrepreneur, podcaster, artist, and community organizer, Betsy created the CampExperience Network, a women's group that hosted events, networking, and annual retreats. Her TEDx Talk, "Choose Your Family, Change Your Life," is all about the lessons she learned while cultivating a chosen family of over 5,000 women over the course of fifteen years. Just as we can learn to come to terms with our family of origin and find home outside of them, we can also cultivate our own chosen family throughout our lives. If there is an expert on how to do that, Betsy is the person to listen to!

Betsy was extremely close with her biological sisters. They stood up for each other. They supported her early entrepreneurial endeavors (like renting her own overalls for $10). She gave her sister a place to stay when her apartment was infected with fleas. And they both sat by her bedside after Betsy was in a life-threatening snowmobile accident and spent twenty-one days in the intensive care unit. Through thick and thin, her sisters were there . . . until Betsy moved from her home of Indianapolis to Denver, Colorado. As her life was taking amazing turns—Betsy was marrying her soul mate, adopting a one-day-old baby girl, and building her network and business from scratch—she felt the absence of her two biggest supporters.

What Betsy did not know was that this end was also a beginning. She started asking, "Where is my tribe?" The people who chose life on purpose, as she did, the ones who felt like her sisters?

With a desire to create the perfect found family, Betsy gathered fifteen friends and brainstormed the question—what would they do if they had two-and-a-half days at "summer camp" where they got to be girls, just like when they were young? The ideas started pouring forth—they would make beaded jewelry, go fly-fishing in pink vests, drink wine, watch movies. But the number one goal was that they would find ways to help other women. Thus, the CampExperience Sisterhood began.

Now, after over fifteen years of CampExperience, with a family of over 5,000 women, Betsy has learned a thing or two about how families of choice come together to form richer, deeper relationships. She told the audience that whether they participate in a club, business, organization, or any other form of chosen family, there are five main ways to cultivate lasting, deep relationships.

Her first tip was to accept that "you get what you get, and you don't throw a fit"—just like with our biological families. Sometimes our family members are awesome and these relationships are close. Other times, depending on the season of your life you are in, you need a different kind of support. Still, Betsy urged, it is important not to turn people away. The word "inclusion" sums up her first tip.

Everyone is invited to the CampExperience, and there is no hierarchy. Betsy explained that she loves the age inclusion aspect. She was in Norway doing a vision-board workshop, and there were people in their twenties and thirties and a woman who was eighty-five. Her name was Agnus. At the start of the workshop, Agnus looked sad. She said, "I do not have any dreams. I have spent my entire life serving others, and I have never taken time for myself."

At first, Betsy did not know what to do, but she did not have to wait long for a solution. Spontaneously, the twenty- and thirty-year-olds gathered next to Agnus and said, "What brings you joy?" She loved flowers. "What brings you happiness?" She said water. The next thing Betsy knew, Agnus had not made just one vision board, but four. This is what inclusion does, Betsy said. It makes a rich mix of perspective and ideas for your family.

The second piece of advice Betsy gave was to be creative because creativity connects us. In this story, she shared that a woman named

Sue came to a fall retreat and announced that she did not enjoy spending time with other women, and she did not know why she was there. Betsy knew the exact remedy. She walked Sue into the craft room and sat her down at a sewing machine. Then, she turned to the sewing volunteer leader, Erlaine, and asked her to teach Sue how to sew a jean jacket.

Another amazing thing started to happen. Sue slowly started to sew and chat, and soften. That hard exterior melted into connection and love. She made a gorgeous jean jacket and stayed in the craft room for the entire weekend. With the right environment, the right supplies, the right instruction, and the right amount of wine, Betsy reassured the audience, anyone can be creative.

The third tip involved a story about a woman named Krista. At a different fall retreat, there was a climbing wall and a zipline. Krista decided it was the perfect time to face her fear of heights. She was terrified to go up that wall . . . but she was even more terrified to let go of all her fears. So Krista gathered her CampExperience™ family—all her sisters—and said she needed them. The sisterhood stood at the bottom of the wall, cheering as Krista ascended. Then, at the very top, she clipped in her harness and launched down the zipline!

Not only did Krista defeat her fear, but she took the whole camp family along for the ride with her. This was Betsy's third lesson: adventure bonds your family of choice.

The fourth piece of advice was to create a safe place to share your voice. By voice, Betsy meant one's innermost dream. Your passion, your purpose—what you really want to do in the world but are just too scared to say aloud. For Betsy, the story of Holly and Eileen captured this power.

Betsy was excited to announce the camp's theme for the following year: "find your voice." There would be a cappella singers, the women would write songs as an exercise, and Eileen said that she wanted to be on the main stage as a speaker. Betsy said, "Awesome, step into your greatness!" and invited Eileen to be a keynote speaker. Eileen practiced, came to the stage, and did an amazing presentation about the joy of being the mother of her daughter, Holly.

Since Holly was a child, she has had one hundred seizures a day. Holly requires 24/7 care, which meant Eileen had to learn how to be a 24/7 advocate for Holly. Holly was also unable to speak. So, at the end of Eileen's powerful talk about sharing your voice, she invited Holly to come forward, then surrounded her on stage with her biological family and her CampExperience™ sisters. They sang "Amazing Grace," surrounding Holly with sound, and those 168 women instantly became family. They were all Holly's sisters. They were all standing with Eileen.

After that experience, the miracles continued. Holly learned to type and shared her thoughts and dreams with others. Through the camp sister partnership, Holly wrote a song and was recorded by Colorado singer-songwriter Megan Burtt and is working on her second book.

The fifth and final tip Betsy shared was "Do good and have fun." She believes there is so much good we can do in the world, and "by focusing not on ourselves, but on what we might do, it changes the world. And it also is a really great bonding agent for your family of choice!"

Finally, Betsy offered three additional secret-sauce elements for building a chosen family: the art of giving and receiving (some people find it easy to give but hard to receive; it just takes practice!);

the art of surprise (planning surprises makes memories, and when you share those surprises, your family bond deepens); and the idea of "happy everything" (like an attitude of gratitude on steroids—being thankful, even when life is hard, because you still have each other. When you focus on what works, you attract more of what works).

In conclusion, Betsy invited the audience to think of how they could cultivate a found family. In fact, consider your life now. Where in your life—your synagogue or church, your school, your company, your activities—can you cultivate powerful relationships? What would be possible if you created an engaged group, had fun, and maybe even changed the world together?

If Betsy's journey is anything of an example, then so much is possible. And so many good things will happen thanks to your chosen family—the people with whom you can truly be yourself. Together, your chosen family makes everyone feel loved and at home, accepted and honored.

The Practice: Where Is Your Center? "I/ME/WE"

When coming home to yourself, it can be useful to identify the various lenses through which you perceive your life. Perception is a mighty tool at our disposal. With this "I/ME/WE" practice, we can start to tune into which "voice" inside of us is speaking at a particular time, then determine which one we *want* to speak into the world. I particularly recommend this practice if you are feeling stuck in old stories about what you can or cannot do, if someone hurt you and you are having a hard time forgiving them, or if you feel like things never go your way. You might find that when you shift your perception, you are able to break through some of these unhelpful stories and find your way home!

In this exercise, consider a situation in which you are struggling. It might be something frustrating that recently happened at work, a difficult conversation with your partner, or a mistake you made that you keep ruminating on, full of self-blame. Use these three pronouns to discern what is going on from three different perspectives.

"I"—This is your ego. It perceives things as happening "to me." It embodies the victim.

"ME"—This is your essence. It perceives things as happening "by me." It embodies the whole self.

"WE"—This is the collective. It perceives things as happening "through me." It embodies trust and flow.

The "I" state is always ego-based; you are a victim of something. Someone did or said something that hurt your feelings. You take it personally, blaming or judging yourself or others. You are reacting to the situation.

In the "ME" state, you become aware of what you are thinking and feeling. You may say, "Yeah, 'they' said or did something that upset me." Yet, you are able to go beyond the victim mentality and see what is actually happening or true for you. Is what they said actually true? Does this situation or person actually support you and your higher self? What is in your best interest as it relates to this situation? From this perspective, you take responsibility for your own feelings and reactions.

The "WE" state is the place where we think through the highest and best path for everyone involved. How can you authentically show up and respond to a situation for the benefit of everyone, yourself included?

"I/ME/WE" is a wonderful practice for breaking out of those self-limiting stories of victimization. We all, at times, get stuck in the "I" state. But, with practice and gentleness, we can continue expanding ourselves out to the "WE," which is where we will find the greatest fulfillment, the healthiest relationships, and ultimately, the most contentment in life.

Oh God of Second Chances, like Dorothy, I had it in me the whole time. Home.

8

Embracing the Divine Feminine

Who is She? She is your power, your Feminine source. Big Mama. The Goddess. The Great Mystery. The web-weaver. The life force. The first time, the twentieth time, you may not recognize her. Or pretend not to hear. As she fills your body with ripples of terror and delight.

But when she calls, you will know you've been called. Then it is up to you to decide if you will answer.
—Lucy H. Pearce, *Burning Woman*

Years ago, back when I worked in sales, I was at a training in Chicago hosted by Nathaniel Branden, PhD, psychotherapist, author, and lecturer. He was a real out-there guy. Interestingly, he was Ayn Rand's former lover and inspired the character John Galt in her seminal book *Atlas Shrugged*. One of the training sessions mentioned an older book from 1979 called *The Invisible Partner: How the Male and Female in Each of Us Affects Our Relationships*, by John A. Sanford.[1] The main premise was something that you might already be familiar with, but it was revolutionary for me at the time: we each have masculine and feminine energies.

I had never known there were two parts of me. But the more I reflected on it, the more it made sense. I had been socialized to be feminine, but when I went out into the larger world, I "armored up" with masculinity. Somewhere along the way, I had learned that my feminine tendencies were not welcomed, especially in the world of my work. I did it as a young kid and also as a young professional. Between the ages of twenty-one and twenty-five, I was traveling to the East Coast to take meetings with big companies. There were times when I was criticized in meetings, and though I was mortified (I was, after all, a punk from Kansas City trying to fit into a very masculine East Coast world), I snapped back with retorts. I did not take shit from anyone, which was how I thought I was supposed to navigate the world.

So, I tucked away my feelings and sensitivity and donned the mask of a woman who does not take things personally. It was my way of meeting society's expectations, but it was also my way of protecting myself. If my softer feminine side was going to be open to judgment or ridicule, then I do not want others to have access to that side of me.

While taking that workshop, I started to realize how much I had rejected an important part of myself. My feminine side was suffering and neglected, and I wanted to reclaim her. That is when an important question took root: how could I show up as my authentic self in all areas of my life?

At the workshop, we were given a workbook called *If You Could Hear What I Cannot Say: Learning to Communicate with the Ones You Love* by Branden.[2] The book is filled with transformational exercises and stem sentences to help you understand who you are, how to improve your communication skills, and how to show up in your relationships. I carried it around for months, reviewing the information and going over the exercises, asking myself how I could find balance between my masculine and feminine energies in my romantic relationships but also to improve my own (life/mental/health/etc.) It was around the same time that I was doing deeper work at the Unity Church. I was starting to see that my satisfaction in life was not about what I did or how much money I made. It had to be about something more. Despite my external success, at the soul level, cutting off half of myself was killing me, and I needed a new way forward.

As fucked up as it sounds, the person with whom I had an affair helped me start exploring my feminine side. He loved my toughness, but he nurtured my feminine side, too, encouraging me to wear lingerie and use products that made me feel sensual. Instead of trying to protect myself, he encouraged me to be more open and engage in a deeper conversation about who I was. Although I crossed so many lines that I deeply regret, it was a powerful journey to start reclaiming my feminine energy. Little did I know, there is more to us than just "masculine" and "feminine," and understanding the distinction makes a big difference.

Pseudo Masculine and Pseudo Feminine

We all have masculine and feminine energies. Like yin and yang, they make up our whole being. And though we might feel that one energy is stronger than the other, it is important to learn how to make space enough for both. No one is complete if they reject part of themselves. Even a seemingly masculine person like actor Dwayne "The Rock" Johnson has feminine qualities that shine when he sings in an animated Disney movie or spends time with kids through the Make-A-Wish Foundation. In the same way, a seemingly feminine person like Kate Middleton, Duchess of

192 | *Oh God of Second Chances*

Cambridge, also embodies masculine qualities to fulfill her duties as British royalty, like offering patronage to many charities. The masculine and the feminine are a spectrum, and we move between the different qualities fluidly, depending on certain situations in life and what they call for.

But our exploration goes even deeper. Masculine and feminine are not only qualities embodied by individuals, but they are also reflected in our larger systems. In Western society, subjects like toxic masculinity have been getting a lot of attention in the last few years. We are grappling with how to have a more just, equal society for women, trans and nonbinary people, and other LGBTQIA+ community members. We are scrutinizing old systems that reflect patriarchal, masculine ideologies, often at the exclusion and demoralization of the feminine.

In these conversations, it is important to be clear: the term "toxic masculinity" does not describe all masculinity as toxic. There is a difference between the pseudomasculine and the divine masculine, just as there is a difference between the pseudofeminine and the divine feminine.

When we are in the pseudomasculine or pseudofeminine, we are really acting out of our reactive tendencies rather than our divine nature. When I first learned about this, I realized that when I "armored up" to go into the work world, I was not donning my divine masculine; I was falling into pseudomasculine behaviors, just as I lived most of my personal life in the pseudofeminine. Understanding the difference between the pseudo and the divine (which I will get to in a moment) is critical to living a full, empowered life of courage and vulnerability, rather than a life of victimhood and "stuckness."

Aspen DeCew, a woman I met when I was leaving the

not-for-profit world, introduced me to energetic re-patterning work. She was a fabulous teacher, coach, and mentor. Her important work informed my understanding of what I now call the Root Causes of life's challenges (our core behavioral patterns that often keep us living small, limited lives), forever changing my life and work. I am incredibly grateful for her contributions. Interestingly, her work did not stop with energy re-patterning. She also created content around masculinity and femininity to help people understand them better, and she is the one who introduced me to the idea of the divine and the pseudo.

As you read the characteristics below detailing divine and pseudo qualities, see if you can identify yourself along the spectrum. Perhaps there are recent instances you can identify where you were operating out of your divine masculine or feminine . . . or your pseudomasculine or feminine.

Pseudo Feminine
Collapsing into emotionality
Collapsing into weakness
Using manipulation
Using sexuality
Indulgence

Divine Feminine
Desire
Flow
Receptivity
Openness
Trust
Vulnerability
Surrender
Allowance
Relaxation

Pseudo Masculine
Forcing
Pushing
Making things happen
Bullying
Fighting
Controlling
Proving

Divine Masculine
Purpose
Presence
Direction
Focus
Clarity
Groundedness
Solidity
Nurturance
Management
Support
Structure
Holding the space
Being the container

It is likely that you have experienced many of the qualities from all of these lists. Only you can know the right balance between your masculine and feminine, but we can all work to live in the divine expression of these traits. When I lived as an "obedient daughter" to my mother, I was operating out of the pseudofeminine, collapsing into that role rather than setting boundaries with my family that represented my needs. Or, when I was burning the candle at both ends and experienced extreme anxiety while taking a suicidal client to the hospital, I was operating out of the pseudomasculine, forcing things to happen in my life rather than having clarity to focus on what was truly needed.

On the other side, as I write this book, I feel a balance within myself between the divine masculine and feminine; I am showing up with direction for what I want to accomplish, and yet I am in the flow of what wants to emerge. It is the perfect balance within my body between confident effort and gentle relaxation and receptivity. This book is an expression of my practice in bringing these energies into harmony.

A Plug without an Outlet

One place in my life that has challenged me to stand in my divine energy—rather than getting lost in the pseudo—is relationships. Especially my marriage.

My husband and I are very different people. I often say that I married the opposite brain. He is logical and technical. He reads legal briefs like nobody's business, whereas I could not give a shit. He is left-brained, analytical, and structured, all qualities which have led to his success as an entrepreneur. By contrast, I am a big-picture thinker, highly conceptual, a little all over the place, and rooted in relationality. Like the story from Chapter 2, he is the brick, and I am the sponge.

As you can imagine, we have had our conflicts over the years. Early on in our relationship, I was operating solely from the pseudofeminine. I took everything personally, and he constantly triggered me. Just like the pseudofeminine qualities listed, I found myself collapsing into weakness and emotionality. Or I would burst out with pseudomasculine reactions—forcing, pushing, or controlling. He was not much better. At times, he could really be a bully. He comes from a family of seven with a highly competitive, intellectual atmosphere. To be heard, he had to be right at all costs. When we fought, he would stubbornly hold his position to the bitter end, until I got to the point of breaking down. When he was in his win-at-all-costs reactive behaviors, it set up a win–lose dynamic, and guess who was always going to lose?

I was struggling with this aspect of our marriage when a therapist introduced me to the idea of a verbally abusive relationship. My first reaction was, "No way, he's not abusive." Then my therapist recommended a book on the subject called *The Verbally Abusive Relationship: How to Recognize It and How to Respond* by Patricia Evans.[3] In the back was a quiz with questions about how to identify if you were in a verbally abusive relationship. It included things like name-calling, if your partner denies the things they have said, or if you always seem to be the one who is blamed when things go wrong. With each question I answered in the affirmative, I felt so seen, like someone was peering into my life. I could not believe how accurate the descriptions in the book were. My quiz score was seven out of ten.

"Holy shit," I thought. "He *is* abusive!"

At the time, I could not wrap my head around it. It is common for highly successful, powerful women to be in verbally abusive relationships. Psychologists and mental health workers cite many varied reasons: abusers like the prestige of high-performing women; these women know how to problem-solve and get results in other areas of their lives, so they think they can do the same in their challenging relationship; and even successful women suffer from self-doubt and insecurities. I cannot tell you how many women I have encountered as a social worker who are in verbally abusive relationships. And now I could not believe I found myself there.

Evans's description of what happens over time in a verbally abusive relationship felt so true: "In a verbally abusive relationship, the partner learns to tolerate abuse without realizing it and to lose self-esteem without realizing it. She is blamed by the abuser and becomes the scapegoat. The partner is then the victim."[4] I knew it was time to get my power back, but I was terrified of talking to my husband. We had a chance to restore our marriage, and despite my fears, if we were successful, I had a feeling it would be beyond worth it.

It ended up being an incredible journey for us, opening up the portal to work together on our communication and reactive behaviors. Over time, we began to change. It was so helpful for me to learn tools that helped me establish boundaries, like saying, "It hurts me when you talk to me that way." I often teach my clients about the idea of an outlet and a plug. When you are embodying a certain energy—like anger or bitterness or blame—you are a plug looking for an outlet. When you find an outlet and plug in, the outlet reacts to your energy, and on some level, you are getting something your ego wants. Maybe it is attention, maybe it is for the other person to feel as bad as you do, or maybe it is to increase your pain so that what you are currently dealing with does not feel as bad. By plugging into their outlet, they join you at the same emotional frequency. As you can imagine, it is ultimately not a healthy scenario for either party.

When we learn to stop being the outlet for other people's negative emotions, we take the wind out of their reactive patterns. They do not get what they are looking for from us, and the responsibility is put back on them to take care of their current experience. A plug without an outlet can poke around in the air all it wants, but if it is not connected to something, it eventually loses steam. This is also a way to think about pseudo and divine feminine and masculine— the pseudo is reacting (plugged into an outlet), and the divine is remaining centered (a plug without an outlet, or no plug at all).

In relationships, we can work together to get out of the plug-and-outlet dynamic and step into our center. I am not saying it is easy, but when we do it, the results are powerful. Early in my marriage, it was like I had multiple outlets available all the time. Until I learned to step into my divine, with incredible results.

Divine Feminine in Action

A story I like to share about the divine feminine in action comes from early in my marriage. I had started my own emotional re-patterning work, learning to unplug from destructive behaviors, but my husband and I were still in our knock-down, drag-out fights. Especially when we were raising our son, Charlie, we were both triggered so easily, and neither of us could handle the other's reactive tendencies.

One night, my husband got upset with me. Instead of fighting with me, he went upstairs and wrote me a letter. The next day, he told me to go upstairs and read it. The letter was not a productive form of communication for our relationship, but rather a collection of his thoughts and feelings from the heat of our fight. As I read it, I remember thinking so clearly, *This does not belong to me. This is his, not mine.* It was not a judgmental or condescending thought, but rather a moment of true clarity from a place of the divine feminine. In that moment, I surrendered to my own awareness, using easy breathing to step into a relaxed state, and chose the divine feminine over my typical reactions (which would have been to retaliate or drink too much).

Calmly, I went downstairs. He was waiting with his plug, charged and spoiling for a fight, but my outlet was nowhere to be seen. With genuine peace in my heart, I said, "I am so thankful you wrote me this letter and that you were willing to express your feelings to me. I do not have anything to say about the contents, but I am happy you shared it with me." I walked away feeling so light and clear, and he had no idea what to do!

When you step out of your reactivity and unplug from others, they can poke at you all day long, but it does not impact you. You are not giving them a charge, and it starts to break your old patterns. This is the power that both the divine feminine and the divine masculine have. They help us, and the people around us, find liberation from our disempowered pseudo patterns so that we can fully embrace our power and potential.

From Pseudo to Divine Masculine

Over the years, I have not only worked on cultivating my divine feminine but also my divine masculine. When I donned my armor as a young professional, it was really the pseudomasculine at work, just as I had operated mostly out of the pseudomasculine in my marriage for a long time. Before my husband and I were able to work together to transform our marriage, I was really at my wit's end. I have a therapist friend who told me about a protocol that couples can use for a trial separation. Basically, you and your partner make an agreement to take a break and do your own personal work, then set parameters around the length of the trial separation and see if your partnership improves.

She gave me the paperwork, and one day, in a fit of frustration, I walked into my husband's office and slapped the papers down on his desk. You can imagine what happened the next morning when he found them! I remember scoffing and saying, "What is the big deal? They are not divorce papers." I would say my behavior at that moment hit almost all the pseudomasculine qualities: forcing, pushing, fighting, controlling.

It was just as important for me to learn to live from my divine masculine as from my divine feminine. I could not keep being passive-aggressive most of the time, then snap into aggressiveness when I had had enough. And though I am writing about the masculine and feminine as if they are separate, they really are not. They work together and become tools we can call upon. When a situation arises that requires our ability to hold space with a soft heart, we can summon the divine feminine. When a situation arises that requires us to stand up for something in a fierce, loving way, we can summon the divine masculine. When we cultivate both in our life, we can move along the spectrum as needed, meeting the unique requirements of each moment, always from a place of strength.

Pseudo Feminine and Energy Vampires

As an Empath (a person who is sensitive to the energies and emotions of others), it took me a long time to understand how people could be so mean. I struggled with my husband's behavior when we would fight and in interactions with coworkers or friends who always made it about them and created endless drama. I often felt misused in relationships, collapsing into pseudofeminine behaviors around others as they took more and more from me.

One day, I listened to a podcast for an emotion-focused therapy summit. Women's health expert and doctor Christiane Northrup was being interviewed about her new book *Dodging Energy Vampires: An Empath's Guide to Evading Relationships That Drain You and Restoring Your Health and Power.*[5] She started to talk about the concept of energy vampires, or people who prey on the compassion of empaths.

Energy vampires are sometimes intentionally manipulative, seeking to use other people for personal gain. They can also be completely oblivious to their tendencies, like friends who always have something to complain about, coworkers who never take personal responsibility for the impact of their actions, or people in your life who use passive-aggressive tactics to put you down and make you feel like you need them. In her book, Northrup defined energy vampires, described how they might show up in your life, and explained how empaths can begin to protect themselves against the drain of someone sucking their energy.

I found her book so impactful that I gave away thirty copies to other empaths in my life. I also asked my husband to read it. He asked if I had given him the book because I thought he was a narcissist. I said, "No, I am not asking you to read this book because of you. I am asking you to read it so you can better understand me as an Empath."

I had witnessed others—myself included—give up their vibrancy and light to people who would drain them dry. It is important to realize that energy vampires actually lack your capacity for empathy. According to Northrup, 20 percent of all people are missing that gene.[6] The spectrum of their behaviors is actually in the manual for psychological disorders, the *DSM-5*. Energy vampires exist somewhere on the spectrum, from narcissistic to sociopathic.

It is challenging for an Empath to be around someone who literally cannot put themselves in another's shoes. For me personally, it has taken stepping out of the pseudofeminine and into my divinity in order to meet that kind of energy. When I am not collapsing into weakness and the emotionality of this person's abuse, I can interact with them from a place of trusting myself and remaining open while maintaining boundaries. The divine feminine helps me remember who I am, and I stop plugging into people whose only agenda is to take and take and take.

It was not until I learned about energy vampires that I really started investigating the relationships in my life. I am a giver, an includer. I want everyone to be involved and feel welcome. I have resources, and I gladly do a lot of things for people. But it took me a while to realize that people will take advantage of generosity. One of the statements in re-patterning work that you can say as a kind of affirmation is "I participate in relationships of mutual giving."

A small example is I used to get the check for every meal. I loved it; my love language is gifts. After reading Northrup's book, I started to see my gifts differently. Some friends were leaning heavily on my generosity, and when I looked closely, I felt like things were out of balance. They would take but offer nothing in return. I have stopped offering to get the cheek every time I eat out with others. It is a sensitive place for me. I love giving, but I also must be careful and assess which relationships really embody mutual giving and which have started to become extractive—all about what the other person can "get."

If you are an Empath, you have a whole other reason to exercise your divine feminine. Your very vitality depends on it. There are those who will take advantage of your generous nature. Let me tell you something: no one is worth sacrificing your own happiness and well-being for.

It Is All about Balance

I was in Mexico years ago with my family. There is a beautiful resort we go to, and various activities are included in the stay. One of the activities that year was painting pre-made ceramics by the pool. I approached the table and saw a ceramic butterfly; immediately, an image came to mind. I had recently participated in a retreat and was mulling over the idea of duality. Playing with dark and light colors, I painted reversed mirror images on each butterfly wing. One side had black on top, the other black on the bottom, and so on. I painted a yin-yang symbol down the middle of the butterfly's body. On the back, I wrote "All of me."

To me, the imagery was a representation of all our pieces coming together. Of wholeness. A butterfly cannot fly with one wing missing, just as we cannot function in a healthy way if we cut off one part of ourselves just because it is not as pretty as the others. I can be a party girl *and* a spiritual girl; an obnoxious, irritable person *and* a responsible, mature human; a person with divine femininity *and* divine masculinity. For so long, I thought these pieces of me were separate—how could I shoot tequila and dance on tables while being spiritual? But that is just a judgment—ours and other people's. When we live in a judgment-free zone, there are no limits to who we can be and all the identities we can combine in order to make up who we are.

This is about both/and not either/or. We all have masculine and feminine energies. We all have pseudo and divine qualities. Even when you are in your most reactive state, you still have divinity in you. And even when you feel the complete unity of the Universe and your illusion of self dissolves, you are still an individual human. This journey is not about escaping one aspect of ourselves because we think it is "bad" or "not spiritual." The journey is about embracing and integrating *all* of us so that we can live whole-heartedly and more skillfully choose which parts of us to bring forward at different times.

The Age of the Divine Feminine

I am a big believer that, on a global scale, the divine feminine is coming through as a rising energy. We have gone into the Age of Aquarius, which is prompting us to step fully into our divinity. For a long time now, our world has been operating from pseudomas culine energy. For many reasons, our social systems and constructs are finally starting to collapse. Just like Daniel Pink observed in the quote I shared in Chapter One, our society is becoming more intuitive, more empathic, and more creative. These skills, which were once seen as "soft," are the same qualities that are actively leading our world in a new direction.

We can see it in our structures, systems, communities, and lives. We see that the system is not working, not only because it is built on pseudo masculinity but also because it excludes the wisdom of the feminine. In truth, we need both, but most of us have not been socialized to appreciate the feminine. Ushering the divine feminine into society starts with women embracing the divine feminine within themselves.

In her book *WomanCode*, holistic health coach Alissa Vitti explores female empowerment through hormone health. In an article on Deepak Chopra's website titled "How to Find the Balance between Your Masculine and Feminine Energy," the author summarized Vitti's findings.

When you are in touch with your divine feminine, you
Magnetically attract what you want
Hold space for projects to develop at their natural pace
Enjoy the process of creation independent of the end result
See the big picture
Work with others and create community
Connect to emotional and physical life as a catalyst for
    change and development
Relate to others by listening, sharing, and nurturing[7]

The divine feminine is powerful. You are able to let go of stories of victimhood and embrace growth. You are able to step into your authenticity, aligning yourself with your essence and your passions.

You are able to do more self-care and get what you want out of life.

The divine feminine has so much to offer us, personally and globally. And it all starts with welcoming it into our lives in a way that is balanced, wholesome, and accepting.

TEDx Feature: Haley Skiko, "How Vulnerability Unleashes Freedom".

Haley Skiko, a twenty-one-year-old senior at the University of Indiana, applied to speak at the 2021 TEDxCherryCreekWomen event. Our team was taken with her youth, her vibrant presence, and her acute awareness of the power of vulnerability.

"Only when we are vulnerable and own our emotions and experiences can we truly feel empowered to live our lives freely and fearlessly." These first words from Haley were so important that she said them twice. Her goal for the talk, she said, was to not only share what those words meant to her, but for them to resonate more deeply with every person in the audience.

At the time of her talk, Haley was about two weeks away from graduating with a degree in business from Indiana University. A big focus in business is interviewing. Whether for a club, job, or internship, being prepared for an interview is important. When Haley was in one of her first mock interviews with a colleague, she was asked a question that she had never been asked before: "What are some of your weaknesses?"

She laughed aloud and said, "Honey, I think you meant to ask my strengths. I am an amazing leader, I am great at time management, and I am super detail-oriented!" The interviewer wore a blank expression and said no, she had meant to ask about Haley's weaknesses. The persistence of the question made Haley defensive. "Why would you want to know about my weaknesses, the things that make me incapable, the things I am bad at? Let me tell you about what I am good at." To this, the interviewer said, "I would argue that your weaknesses are what make you most capable because they make you aware and accountable."

The minute she heard this, something sparked in Haley. She had to reflect on why she always associated weakness—showing outward vulnerability—with something negative. Going back to her roots, she had grown up with women who were strong and driven, who showed nurture and care and love on the outside. Even expressing positivity can be stifling. No matter what was going on inside, these women displayed light, love, and happiness to others. Haley, following that example, had always been giving to whoever needed something, no matter how she was feeling inside. She finally paused to ask herself the following question—if she was busy anchoring everyone around her, was she anchored in herself?

The answer, she realized, was no. This realization forced her to step back and wonder why we constantly avoid our weaknesses instead of owning them. Everyone has their own excuses and barriers that prevent them from processing challenging emotions. As an example, especially for women, is that when someone compliments us—*that was an amazing event; you look so good today; you are so amazing*—our innate response is to deflect the compliment. *I look awful,* or *you look so much better,* or *I wish I had done better.* Immediately, we invalidate ourselves until we feel completely insecure inside.

Haley's personal questioning deepened—she wondered what barriers she had erected in her own life. It turned out they had to do with minimizing her pain in comparison to the pain of others. If other people had experienced greater hardships, why did she deserve to process the pain she felt? She preferred to help everyone else with their pain because she had decided that hers did not matter as much.

This really hit when she was sixteen years old. On a random day in August, her parents sat her down at the kitchen table with her siblings and said they were getting divorced. At first, Haley thought it was a joke. Her father reassured her and her siblings that it was a good situation—the kids were going to stay in the same home, and Haley's mom and dad were going to move back and forth. They were still going to have family dinners on Sundays, and her mom and dad were still best friends.

Half of her wondered if she should cry in happiness because her parents were still best friends and were going to make it work, and half of her wanted to cry tears of devastation because the people she had known as a couple for twenty-one years were now going to be apart. Because of that split, Haley invalidated her own experience. She did not want to process the complicated feelings, so she suppressed them. When someone asked her if she was okay, she reassured them that she was good. After all, she had a friend whose parents' financial problems led to divorce, friends who did not have a relationship with their parents because of divorce, and friends who did not even know their parents well because of divorce. In comparison, Haley thought her situation was not nearly as bad, so it did not deserve to be validated.

Haley said that if we do not validate our own pain and process it, allowing it to be ours, we not only keep our true self from others, but we show other people what we want them to see rather than what is true. It all comes down to whether we have validated our own pain and gone through our own unique process of healing.

Our culture of showing strength and positivity and light on the outside has a dark edge. If we are really crumbling on the inside, this dynamic can hurt our relationships and ourselves. This became clear to Haley in her relationship with her little sister. After four years apart, they were not always the closest, and they were extremely different women. Haley was a passionate doer; her sister was a systematic thinker. To explain their dynamic, Haley shared that when she was going through something or struggling, her sister would say, "Haley, relax. We get it, you are a Capricorn."

About a year and a half prior, her sister had been diagnosed with severe depression and anxiety, which reached the point of suicidal thoughts. "When someone you love so much is going through something like that, something breaks in you. Something broke in me."

Haley did not know how to help her sister, and she did not know how to feel, so she did the only thing she knew how to do. She showed up with that strong, passionate, positive light of hers. She told her sister about all the amazing things Haley was doing in school and all the things her sister was going to do, bringing all kinds of motivational energy.

As a result, she found that her relationship with her sister was more distant than ever. There was a wedge between them, and she did not understand why—until one day, she broke down. In her crying and vulnerable state, Haley said to her sister, "I do not know how to help you, but I love you and I want to walk with you." Her sister smiled and said, "Haley, that is what I have wanted." Her sister told Haley that by showing up as her genuine self that day—not in the way she thought she should—it helped.

With this insight, Haley said, "The people that we love and the people that love us will accept us, no matter how we show up that day." It takes feeling secure inside to feel confident on the outside, especially when we know that people will continue to love and embrace us. Sharing our vulnerabilities helps us own our identity and express who we really are.

Her sister's journey to happiness taught Haley that it is okay to show people how you are truly feeling. We really have two sides, Haley said—our weaknesses and losses, and our strengths and wins. Both halves deserve to be recognized and honored. Our weaknesses help us grow, and our strengths help us give ourselves credit. None of us can be 100 percent "on" all the time, but if we are 100 percent authentic inside, others will know we are always showing up as ourselves, all the time.

In closing, Haley asked people to consider how they can own who they are to a greater extent so they can better help themselves and the people around them. She now knew that her weaknesses made her aware and accountable and that they had taught her how to be better.

Haley's talk came full circle as she returned to her first statement: "Only when we are vulnerable and own our emotions and experiences can we truly feel empowered to live our lives freely and fearlessly." To anyone who felt weak, struggling, or in pain, Haley reassured them that that is what made them strong, if they allowed themselves to process, heal, and learn from those situations.

Haley's talk, to me, is the embodiment of the divine feminine. It is about finding our strength in our vulnerabilities; it is leading with our relationship with ourselves first; it is tapping into what is true inside rather than what we think people want to see outside. By living from this place of soft strength, as Haley suggested, we can come more fully into who we are, and we can also show up more fully in our relationships.

The Practice: Cultivating the Divine Feminine

A sentence stem is a wonderful tool that gives structure to ideas and learning. You may know it from school—you are given the start of a sentence, and you complete it.

Using the list of divine feminine qualities from the start of the chapter, complete the following sentence stems. By defining how you want these qualities to permeate your life, you create an intention that you can work toward. You can repeat a sentence stem as many times as you wish. Trust the process, trust yourself, and trust what comes through!

I Desire . . .
I Flow . . .
I am Receptive . . .
I am Open . . .
I Trust . . .
I am Vulnerable . . .
I Surrender . . .
I am Allowing . . .
I Relax . . .

For example,

I desire a healthy relationship.
I desire freedom to express myself.
I flow in the direction of my divine energy.
I am receptive to abundance.
I am receptive to tons of fun.
I am open to change.
I trust the divine.
I am vulnerable (very!).
I surrender to the illusion of control.

I am allowing the unfolding of my life's work.
I relax, let go, and let God!

Oh God of Second Chances, May I embrace the unfolding of the divine feminine in and around me. May I trust her to guide me to my highest and best self.

9

Being a Woman in Today's World

"There is nothing more powerful than a woman who has wiped away her own tears and risen from everything sent to destroy her. You will never find her chasing anyone nor seeking external validation. She won't tolerate drama or bullshit. She knows herself and that is all that matters."
—Marianne Williamson

A woman must have money and a room of her own if she is to write fiction.
—Virginia Woolf, *A Room of One's Own*

Sick of Being a Woman

"I thought you liked those things," he said in our therapy session. Years ago, my husband and I were going to therapy and working through our challenges. In one session, I brought in a letter. I have been journaling every day for years, and this journal entry was salty. The entire piece was about how I did not like being a woman because it was so damn hard.

This was the first he had heard about it. "What do you mean?" he asked, bewildered by the thought that I might not enjoy being a woman. Oh-ho! Did I have a list for him! "Who likes getting their hair colored every month?" I erupted. "Or their fingernails and toes painted? Shaving legs and armpits, waxing 'parts.' What about bras? Do you know how it feels to wear a bra on a regular basis? And don't get me started on periods and childbirth!"

It is amazing the stories we adopt of what a "woman" looks like in the world based on our upbringing and particular exposure to society. My emotional tipping point was brought on by my own insecurities and my desire to blame my husband for my shit. Of course, it was not really his fault. I had committed myself to what I thought were the "right" ways to be a woman and a wife in the world. I had never mentioned that I found these aspects of my life tedious (and painful), nor had I paused to consider that I had a choice in the matter. Nobody was forcing me to do these things, and yet I had become so dedicated to my false identity, showing up to events looking and acting a certain way. Over time, instead of taking ownership of my actions or choosing different priorities, I allowed resentment to brew. I blamed my husband and the world for my choices.

I always think of an interview I listened to with Kristin Richard, Lance Armstrong's first wife. When they married, she took his name and quickly felt her identity erode. She had been successful in her own right, working for an advertising and public relations firm. She was beautiful, successful, and multilingual. Then she married Lance. Her identity morphed into what she thought was the "right" role as his wife and the mother of their children. Since their divorce, she has written and spoken about that journey and her way back to herself.[1]

Richard's story is so familiar to many women. We are so easily defined by our roles at different points in our lives—girl, young adult, girlfriend, working woman, wife, mother, working mother, empty nester, crone. Whether it is our age, the roles we are filling, or our current activities, we are supposed to buy into labels—these limiting ideas about who we truly are at our core. In hindsight, I had it easy. For a lot of women, these dynamics are much more complicated and challenging.

I always thought of myself as a self-sufficient, competent woman, and I was. But there was something about the early years of my marriage that made me think that I had to be something or someone other than who I was in order to be acceptable. It was not always like that. Before I married and moved to Denver, I owned a three-bedroom home with a main floor primary bedroom. Because I traveled so much for work, I rented the upstairs bedrooms. Just prior to moving to Denver, I had a great guy who rented a room from me. He cleaned the house, walked the dog, and cooked for me. I never ironed and took everything to the dry cleaner. I had built a life I loved as an independent woman. And yet, when I married, I bought into all these new labels that I associated with "wife." And I let them fester until I ultimately felt like being a woman in today's world kind of sucked.

If you have ever felt this way, or you have struggled to know who you are independent of the labels your community or society has put on you, you are not alone. In fact, some of these dynamics are deeply embedded in our ideas of safety and inclusion. We all want to feel like we belong, which sometimes means we purposefully hold ourselves—and each other—back from our truest expressions.

The Crab Bucket

I have written a lot about how we are influenced by our family dynamics growing up, but we are also influenced by our culture. Our culture is the water we swim in, and it can be unique to each person. For many of us, it is scary to go against cultural norms. The animal part of our brain wants us to remain part of the group and avoid standing out in a negative way that might lead to our expulsion from the community; there is safety in numbers. These dynamics can make it even harder to determine who we are as women today. Worse, sometimes we hold each other back from living to the fullest because we think we are keeping each other safe.

If you have been crabbing before, you might have seen this. If you put a single crab in a bucket, it will muster all its tiny might to scramble out. However, when two or more crabs are put into a bucket, they make it even more difficult for each other to get out. Rather than help each other up, they pull each other down.

As a social worker for ten years before becoming a women's leadership and empowerment coach, I have seen this over and over in my career. The systems designed to help individuals and families often fail them and function to keep people stuck. Once in "the system," it takes significant courage—among other things—to get out, especially for families in poverty.

Multigenerational poverty is hard to break out of. Even when new opportunities present themselves, they can feel disorienting to navigate, especially if no one in your immediate family has provided an example. My brother's children come to mind. They had a tough upbringing, and two of them were put into foster care when their parents were not able to provide a stable environment. Both were given incredible opportunities. They had full-ride scholarships for school—my niece was in cosmetology school, and she was so brilliant at it, but she did not have the bandwidth to finish. She is now a single mom and reaching out for help. My nephew did not complete school either. He struggles in his daily life to survive and thrive. My youngest niece was also brought up in a challenging environment. I was able to step in when she was sixteen and my mother was no longer able to care for her. With the advice of a professional, we arranged for her to attend a wilderness therapy program and then a program that enabled her to graduate high school. She was set to go to college, but she found it too difficult. She went back to her hometown with her friends. Now, she is nineteen, pregnant, and living in poverty.

Sometimes it is easier to allow yourself to be pulled back into the crab bucket. It is familiar. Plus, when we work to climb out of the crab bucket, it makes the other crabs uncomfortable. Whenever I visited Kansas after moving to Denver, there was an uncomfortable tension. My family was supportive of my unique direction—graduating from high school, putting myself through college, working two jobs—but my mom would still question my choices. Deep down, I think she wanted me to move back to Kansas and do "normal" things that she understood. I did not have it in me to stay in that bucket, but for so many people, it is easier to stay in the middle, crabbing it out, even if it means not living up to their potential.

I have even witnessed this among powerful, successful, high-profile women. It is much easier to stay in the crab bucket than it is to develop and grow. Most of this "sticking to the status quo" is driven by fear. We fear being judged. We fear coming across as frauds. We fear growing too tall just to be chopped down. We are afraid of being misunderstood, rejected, or unappreciated, so we stay small and scared, telling ourselves that we are safe. Until one day, when we hopefully realize that our perceived sense of safety is not worth sacrificing the opportunity to live fully. No one wants to get to the end of their life to look back and see so much potential, opportunity, and vibrancy left on the table.

But if the crab bucket and our culture are deeply intertwined, how do we know when we are in a crab bucket? And how do we know when we have successfully climbed out?

Everyone's Crab Bucket Looks Different

The crab bucket looks different for everyone. Sometimes circumstances are truly hard to overcome, but that doesn't mean you cannot live a life of internal freedom. Only you will know what a crab bucket looks like in your life. I have seen some people who, from the outside, seem to have it all. But inside, they are playing by everyone else's rules, and they are miserable. On the other hand, I have known people whose lives look really challenging from the outside—they may even seem stuck and destined to repeat the same patterns—but they follow their own inner voice and are happier for it.

This brings to mind the story of a woman named Carol. She had a deep influence on my life, and though her story is full of joy, it also contains unimaginable heartbreak. Her life and story shaped me in more ways than I can say.

As you know, my mom had a way of bringing home strangers (remember the Thanksgiving with my family plus everyone from the local bar?). I remember, when I was very young, Mom once brought home a boy—a very cute boy, I might add—and said he would be living with us. I am not sure why. He only lasted about a week or so, and then he was gone. It was an odd dynamic, but sometimes she brought home really interesting people.

One day when I was in junior high, my mom brought home a woman named Carol. They worked together at the bowling alley.

Carol had a slight build and a lovely character. She made our basement her home. She had a large collection of forty-five records, and she was generous in letting me use them. "Stop, wait a minute, Mr. Postman," I would sing at the top of my lungs. It was a song by the Carpenters, and it was the bubblegum music of the era. I loved it. I would sing and dance to her records for hours. One time I put on my pink genie outfit, then blasted "Devil with a Blue Dress On," dancing across the basement like a maniac. It took me a few minutes to notice my family at the top of the stairs, laughing their asses off as they watched.

Carol drove a gray-colored Charger. It was the coolest car I had ever seen. I would ride in it with her to the QuikTrip gas station to buy smokes and Diet Coke. I had never felt so cool in my life.

Carol dated while she lived with us, which meant there was never a dull moment. One night, I was lying in my bed when I heard a lot of commotion. My room was the closest to the front of the house, and my window opened to our large front porch with a view of busy 83rd Street. When I lifted the shade to see what was going on, Carol's boyfriend was sitting in his car across the street. He stayed there for hours, watching our house. Feeling the tension, I stayed awake, wondering what was going to happen. It all seemed so dramatic. But, as is the plight of a kid, I ultimately fell asleep, and life went on.

Carol then started dating a guy named Lawrence. He was beautiful, and they seemed very much in love. They married and moved just four doors down from us. My relationship with Carol continued while she lived there. She called me "Sis," and I really did come to see her as an older sister.

Carol started working for a meatpacking plant and split her time between the Kansas City and Topeka offices. I even visited her at the plant one day. The sight of skinned cows on meat hooks hanging from the ceiling was strange and disturbing. I believe my parents chose a side of beef to be brought home and stored in our freezer that day. Sometime after our visit, Carol was driving her Charger down I-70 on her way to Topeka. She saw someone hitchhiking on the side of the road and thought she recognized him. She pulled over and let him in realizing he was not who she thought she recognized.

As the story went, he pulled a knife and instructed her to drive off onto a dirt road. Once out of sight from the road, he raped, beat, tortured, and robbed her, running her over with the Charger before leaving her for dead.

Fortunately, by the grace of God, she was able to crawl far enough toward the highway that a school bus driver spotted her and called the police. She was found and taken to the hospital. Her injuries were serious, and her emotional trauma was something she would face for the rest of her life.

When I saw Carol again, the whites of her eyes were still red from the severe, brutal beating. She was frail. Lawrence did his best to be supportive. Their marriage did not survive.

One of the biggest challenges for Carol was not just the trauma of her assault or the loss of her marriage, but being told she would never be able to have children after the attack. But she was tough. She hung in there, and her perpetrator was found and prosecuted. Carol ended up moving to a small town in Missouri. She met a lovely guy and got pregnant with her miracle baby. My family went to visit after her son was born.

I lost touch with Carol until I was around thirty. She had moved to another small town just north of Kansas City, and I went to visit.

She was bar tending, still smoking, and single, and she'd had a falling out with her beloved miracle child and was not in touch with him. It was hard to see her all by herself. But she was Carol. She loved me, and I loved her. We partied the night away, sharing old stories and reminiscing about the time when she lived in my home.

Ultimately, Carol died of lung cancer. There was no funeral. I have always held Carol deep in my heart and feel blessed to have known her. A fierce survivor, my sis, she fought for her life. Most people could not survive all the trauma she experienced that day and in the months and years after. Some would see Carol as a victim, but I see her as a survivor. I see someone who fought to keep living in the best ways she knew how. No one was going to keep her down or in a crab bucket.

Getting out of a crab bucket does not mean you are able to craft an entirely new life for yourself. It means you are free of internal and external expectations and able to make your own decisions about how to navigate your life, whatever that looks like. At the end of the day, only you can decide what getting out of the crab bucket looks like for you and if you are willing to take those steps.

Women Pulling Each Other Down

Sadly, in our society, women are often pitted against each other. Because our place has not been equal compared to men, our opportunities for succeeding are perceived as limited. We come to believe that other women are competition, whether it is for a promotion or even a partner. These kinds of dynamics are embedded everywhere, like in the stories we consume.

In the last twenty years, we have finally become more critical of how women are portrayed in the media. How many stories have we read or seen that show women as adversaries, particularly over a male love interest? The Bechdel test measures the representation of women in fiction. Proposed by American cartoonist Alison Bechdel, the test looks at movies and other works of fiction and asks if there are two female characters who interact about something not related to a man (according to public data, about half of the films pass the test).[2] The Bechdel test doesn't necessarily get into the nuances of proper representation of women in media, but it does ask an important question regarding how female relationships are commonly portrayed. What kind of influence does this have on our psyche as women?

Over the last few decades, fascinating research has emerged about female bullying. Apparently, what was portrayed in the hit movie *Mean Girls* is not too far from the truth of what some women experience. Women are very relationship-oriented, which is exactly the dynamic female bullies target. Whether we are at school, in the workplace, with a mom's group, or at yoga, we might encounter different forms of "relational aggression."[3] In a *Psychology Today* article, psychologist Nicki R. Crick said, "For the past three years we have been looking at the ways girls try to harm others. We have identified a form of aggression unique to females, what we call relational aggression, hurting others through damaging or manipulating their relationships in aversive ways."[4] This could include things like being rejected or shunned, being manipulated in order to receive approval, or being humiliated through teasing or gossip.

You may have been subjected to types of relational bullying throughout your life, or maybe you've been a perpetrator before you knew better. Part of our role in healing our relationships with other women includes investing in inner work. Bullying often comes from a place of hurt, insecurity, and fear. If we are not able to step outside of our own labels and the ways in which we feel limited, we are not only likely to inflict harm on ourselves but on others, too. We become the crabs, holding other people down under the illusion that it will make us feel better about our own lives.

Taking a Spiritual Women's Weekend

When my son Charlie was twelve, I decided that I wanted to take him on an RV trip to the Grand Canyon. We were going to drive through Yellowstone and see all the sights. When I told my husband, he said, "I am not going on an RV trip. You drive. I will fly and meet you when you stop." I was not happy and could not understand why he would not want to take this road trip with us, but I decided to proceed anyway.

Ten days before we were supposed to leave, he came to me with a whole itinerary for our RV trip, including where he would meet us along the way. Instead of seeing this as an act of service or his way of helping, I lost it! I said, "Hell no! You are not the one controlling this." It was not my most divine feminine moment either, and one of the biggest fights of our marriage ensued.

In the end, he joined us. Charlie, our dog Lucky, my niece, my husband, and I set out on our twelve-day trip. My husband managed to secure a brand-new RV for us. It was one of the cheesy ones, with decals of fake kids hanging out the windows. To add to the cheesy experience, I played Willie Nelson's "On the Road Again" every time we departed—at which everyone in the RV rolled their eyes.

We headed north from Denver to Wyoming. We spent our first night in a campground and settled in to watch a beautiful sunset. From Wyoming, we headed east to the Dakotas, where we saw Mount Rushmore and Devils Tower, the site made famous by the movie *Close Encounters of the Third Kind*. Back West, we went to Yellowstone National Forest and visited Old Faithful. We visited friends in West Yellowstone, then headed back the way we came to the Grand Tetons and through Cody, Wyoming, to attend the famous Cody Rodeo. Charlie did mutton busting; it was so damn cute watching him running around, trying to wrangle that little sheep. It was an incredible and memorable trip, with beautiful, amazing sights.

In hindsight, we should have stayed a night or two at hotels to give us a break from the close proximity to each other in the RV. According to my husband, I snore, so he did not get much sleep. Four people and a dog living that close for that long . . . Well, just let me reiterate: we should have had a few nights in hotels.

Another thing I did for the trip was plan plenty of games and activities for the kids and create music playlists for the drive. I also love listening to educational materials in the car, so I went to the library and checked out audio tapes of Joan Borysenko, a Harvard-trained doctor, author, and speaker. She had these spiritual women's weekend talks on tape. This one in particular was about a woman's journey through her life and what happens to her over time physically, psychologically, and spiritually.

While we drove in the RV, I listened. Borysenko said that when we reach age forty or fifty (I was the latter as I listened), the kids are typically grown and out on their own. We become empty nesters, and a lot of changes happen. Psychologically, we are done taking care of everyone else. In some ways, we are biologically designed to care for and support others. But it is an arduous journey, and we get tired of it. By this point, we are just done. Physically, we start to go through menopause. Our testosterone goes up, and our estrogen goes down. In a way, we step more fully into our masculinity, and we are now defined by all the times we set boundaries and declare, "Hell no!" Spiritually, we start seeking something for ourselves beyond the roles and activities we have engaged in up until this point.

It is not uncommon, she said, for women to experience divorce at this age. When a woman is done being the caregiver, the people around her who have grown accustomed to that role are shocked by the changes. Children and partners can feel confused. They have leaned on the woman to take care of so much in their lives. These changes are natural, and it is important for our society to support women as their roles and identities shift over time.

All of this culminates in a transformation. Some know it as a "midlife crisis." It can certainly feel like a crisis as we let go of our familiar identities. But on the other side of those labels is so much freedom. We are awakening to a greater self. When we set down "working mother," "partner," "wife," or "booster club president" and all the expectations that go along with our labels, we can just *be*. And we might find that we are capable of so much more than anyone knew, especially ourselves.

You Are Not What You Do

It is our job to get beneath the labels that others put on us and we put on ourselves. You are not what you do. You have a being, an essence, which is your eternal guide to your destiny. We all go through different developmental stages. This is healthy. But it is just as important to know that those labels are not who we are.

I see this so much in my friends and clients who are highly successful in the corporate world. They start approaching retirement, or, God forbid, they get laid off because of unexpected circumstances. Without their position, they do not know who they are anymore or what value they have in the world. They feel adrift, lost, even depressed, as if their successful job were all they were good for.

Or, for some, it is the identity of being a mother. A lot of moms in my world are becoming empty nesters. Just this week, a friend is sending her daughter to college, and she is beside herself. She does not know who she is without her kids and her role as a mom. Never mind that she, and these other women, are incredibly talented and offer so much to the world. They just cannot see past the identity disruption.

This all goes back to the discussion about remembering and forgetting in Chapter Four. Remember that you are already whole and complete, no matter what. No number of changing labels can take that away. It does not matter what you do, how old you are, where you came from, what your family does or does not do—none of those matters. All that matters is that you have some way of connecting to your higher self and knowing that you are so much more than what you do or the roles that you play in this life.

Rewriting the Story of Aging

Our society has such twisted ideas about aging, especially for women, that it is worth addressing here. Let me start by saying: I *love* aging. I use this mantra every time I am reminded of my actual age—*I love* aging. Like when I walk into the hair salon for that oh-so-fun process of having my gray roots colored. Or when I try to get off the floor and need a hand to lift me up. Or when I stand after sitting for a bit at my computer and think, *Oh shit, that hurts*, and I walk out of my office hoping my legs do not give out.

The list goes on. Yet, aging has its advantages—yes, my back hurts, yes, my knees crack, but I see my life more clearly than I ever have. Gone are the days of youthful insecurity and fear. The older I get, the more I sink into the reality of who I am and what I am here to do. There is a gift in getting closer to the end; you realize how precious it all is and that you really have no time to waste on frivolous things like self-doubt.

I am passionate about rewriting our cultural norms about women and aging. Remember the Sage Moms I met when I was eighteen? Well, when these women turned sixty-five, I hosted a croning ceremony for them. The crone is an ancient symbol that is part of the triple goddess—maiden, mother, and crone. Together, they represent the circle of life. The crone is the final stage a woman passes through. She is the wise woman, the grandmother, the embodiment of winter. Whereas modern Western society sees old women as a kind of burden, in other cultures, including ancient ones, the elderly are often viewed with great respect.

I wanted to honor these women. I wanted to reflect back on who they were to me and to each other. At this point, one of the women had passed away. Having attended her funeral and witnessed the beautiful stories that were shared, I knew in my bones that I did not want the people in my life to only hear how important they were at their funerals. I wanted them to know *now*, while we were all living, instead of us waiting to memorialize each other.

For the ceremony, we all went to a mountain house in Winter Park, Colorado, and we shared a weekend of love and laughter. The theme I chose was "cowgirl." I hired some folk singers from Denver to perform one night, and I led activities like journaling and deep conversations. I had the women get clear about their desires and what they wanted to manifest in their lives going forward. We made vision boards out of magazine clippings, and I added glitter and sparkles to bring some pizzazz. They loved the rituals, and we had so much fun laughing and letting go.

In fact, one of my favorite stories ever came from that weekend. It was my turn to cook, so I went to the store to get groceries for a good old-fashioned steak dinner, as well as a birthday cake. I returned feeling a bit stressed because of the logistics and surprises I had planned. When I opened the garage to pull in the car to unload the groceries, my Sage Moms were there in a semicircle, wearing their bras and underwear outside their clothes, doing the can-can. Unbelievable! I never knew what would happen next with these girls. That was basically our whole weekend together—laughter, heart, ceremony, and the embrace of friends.

We celebrated birthdays that evening, and I gifted them each a wooden plaque that said, "Pull up your big girl panties and deal with it." I keep the picture of them in their undergarments and this plaque next to each other and laugh every time I see them.

On the night before we were all to depart, we went to a beautiful ranch property called Devil's Thumb, just down the road from my Winter Park home. There, I hosted a croning ritual for them—a ceremony in which women are honored in the third stage of life, age sixty and older. The ceremony included reflection, laughter, drumming, singing, dancing, and sharing rich life stories. We shared the deep appreciation we felt for each other and the blessings that each of us had received from the others. This was one of the most powerful experiences of my life. I love these women beyond measure and am so blessed that they have allowed me into their family. I will author another book one day about the many journeys of love, friendship, and family this group has given me.

As you encounter transitions in your life—especially difficult ones—I would encourage you to create ceremonies to commemorate them. Invite your like-minded friends to participate or co-create the event together. Ceremonies can be a beautiful way to shed old layers (including labels!), heal the parts of ourselves that remain wounded, and step into the world with fresh inspiration in our hearts. Especially as women in today's world, we deserve as much, and so much more.

TEDx Feature: Gretchen Gagel, "The Power to Change the Working Mom Conversation".

I met Gretchen Gagel when I was working at a not-for-profit organization. She was the president of The Women's Foundation of Colorado. We were part of a public policy collaboration that was working to improve policy for women with low incomes who were moving from welfare to work. I was a bit intimidated by her at first. Unbeknownst to me, she was also a Kansas girl, and we were from the same area. Our friendship has blossomed over the years, and I have had the privilege of traveling with her and watching her continued successes in so many ways. Her TEDx Talk is based on her book, *The Eight Steps to Being a Great Working Mom*, and it is a great reflection on being a woman in today's world—especially as a working mother.

Gretchen's talk started with a snippet of conversation: "Have you started looking for Gretchen's replacement yet?" Imagine her surprise at hearing those words spoken by a client to her boss at a cocktail party—with her standing right there. The client did not say it because Gretchen was not doing a good job or because she was leaving to work for a competitor. He said it because she was pregnant.

Twenty years prior, Gretchen had been living a very happy, exciting life, working as a management consultant. When she learned she was pregnant with her first child, she was really nervous about telling her boss. Her firm worked in construction. There were about seventy consultants, of whom two were women. Gretchen traveled about four days out of the week, and she did not have many role models of other mothers who had made this kind of job and lifestyle work.

Finally, she got up enough nerve to tell her boss that she was pregnant. He was supportive, telling her they would make it work. But it was not just his input that impacted her. People around her started saying things that slowly eroded her self-confidence, making her question her choice. After telling her boss about these occurrences, he waved it off, saying she was imagining things and reading too much into what people were saying.

She thought he was right until that night at the cocktail party. After the question was posed, Gretchen stayed silent, sensing that this client had more to contribute. To her horror, she was right.

The client went on to say to her, "These yearnings that were put in you to be a mother will overpower these feelings that you have of wanting a career." Basically, the client was telling her that she would "come to her senses" and figure out where she belonged: at home with her kids, not building a career.

Thinking about this story even years later, Gretchen felt a pit of anger in her stomach. There she was, young and expecting her first child, already afraid to think about becoming a mom, especially given she had never even put a diaper on a baby. Who was this man to say these things to her and make her feel this way?

Gretchen knew she was not alone in this kind of experience and used her story to highlight a huge problem in our country. Seventy percent of women with children under the age of eighteen participated in the workforce. However, a third of the women surveyed felt that women with children should not work. The statistics highlight a huge disconnect between reality and what many people believe.

Since publishing her book, *The Eight Steps to Being a Great Working Mom*, Gretchen has spoken with hundreds of women about their stories. She recalled recently sitting next to a woman on a plane who was a single mom with a ten- and fifteen-year-old. Every day, this woman picked up her kids from school and brought them to her office where they had a desk, and she helped them with their homework while finishing her own work. A school official told the woman that her son would be doing better in school if she did not work so much.

Or, in another story, a woman came up to Gretchen at a book signing. The woman was pregnant with her third child, and an office mate had recently said to her, "You've been barely hanging on with two; you can kiss your career goodbye with three."

It is these kinds of toxic conversations that add complexity and difficulty to being a woman in today's world. But hope is not lost. As Gretchen said, we have the power to change the conversation. And it starts with how we speak to each other.

Instead of common conversational phrases like "Is your husband going to let you keep working?", what if we said, "What a great role model you will be for your kids." Instead of saying, "Do you think you will be able to keep working after the baby?", what if we said, "You will make the choice that is right for you, and you will make it work." Instead of "How did your kids turn out?"—like they were raised in a science experiment—what if we said, "I bet you have wonderful kids who appreciate all the things you do for them." Instead of "It must be a challenge to work and take care of your family," what if we said, "I admire how you juggle work and taking care of your family and your career."

And now for my personal favorite: Gretchen's salty response to the question, "Who watches your kids when you are gone?" Gretchen heard this one every week for about ten years, and she grew so tired of it that she chose to use humor to deflect it. Her response was, "You know what, I put them in the trunk of my car with a little food and water, and so far, it seems to be working out just fine!"

Gretchen declared that we have the power to change the conversation and to be supportive of working moms. But she made an important distinction—not only does the conversation around working moms need to change, but also the conversation *inside the heads* of working moms.

Working moms, she said, "Need to let go of unrealistic

expectations that cause stress and guilt. Somehow, we have decided that on any given day we need to be Warren Buffett and Heidi Klum and Martha Stewart, all wrapped up into one. It is not realistic."

She encouraged every working mom to think about an expectation they needed to let go of—common stories like "All school snacks need to be homemade" or "Sure, I can take on ten extra projects at work." Using the help of a small notepad and a garbage can, Gretchen symbolically wrote every unrealistic expectation on a piece of paper, then promptly balled it up and threw it away. It was an invitation to working moms to be easier on themselves because they already put so much into everything they do.

Bringing it full circle, Gretchen concluded by pondering what it would have been like if that client had instead turned to her and said, "You are going to make a great mom." It would have made all the difference—not only in her life, but in the broader culture of how we treat women in our world.

With a final slide displaying images of her two kids at their respective graduations, Gretchen showed the audience what a working mom really looks like: smiling beside her kids, proud, enjoying the greatest gift of her life—*that* is motherhood.

M—Master	M—Most	M—Magician
O—Open	O—Organ	O—Out
T—Thoughtful	T—Tough	T—Trustworthy
H—Hard	H—Herding	H—Hindered
E—Either	E—Ever-present	E—Expansive
R—Or	R—Remembers	R—Responds
H—Helpful	H—Hopeful	H—(w)Holly
O—Opinionated	O—Ordained	O—Omni-everything
O—Organized	O—Obedient	O—Organized
D—Dominate	D—Dormant	D—Darn right

The Practice: Digging into the Layers of Being a Woman

Acronyms are a powerful way to explore what might be going on in your subconscious mind. I have used them for years to reflect on people and situations in my life. The MOTHERHOOD acronym above and the WOMAN acronym below show an example of what this practice might look like.

Choose a word related to your experience of being a woman in today's world. It could be "WOMAN," "MOTHERHOOD," "SISTER," or "WIFE." Whatever one you choose, write that word down three times, then fill out the acronym using different words each time. Let your word choices flow; do not think about them too much.

Here are three acronyms for the word "WOMAN":

W—Wounded
O—Open
M—Male-dominated
A—Advancing
N—Nice

W—Wise
O—Ovaries
M—Maternal
A—Angelic
N—Now is the time

W—Wonder
O—Options
M—Magnetic
A—Amazing
N—Neutral

After you complete the acronym practice, reflect on the three word sets and write a brief sentence about what you see. Here is an example:

This first set of words will most likely reflect your unconscious thoughts: *As a woman, I am wounded, male-dominated, and too nice, and I am open and advancing.*

The second group of words will likely indicate the direction you feel yourself moving on your good days: *I am wise, maternal, and angelic; now is the time to bring my best self.*

The third group of words will likely represent what you aspire to be: *I am magnetic, amazing, and full of wonder and options. I am neutral (non-judgmental).*

I find that acronyms are a powerful tool for any issue that I am pondering. Especially as we expand our definitions of what it means to be a woman in today's world—and as we release that which we no longer want to hold—this practice can peel back those hard-to-reach layers of our identity and set a course for what is next!

Oh God of Second Chances, may I embrace the experience of being a woman in today's world as I am.

10

Healing Through Service

The simple path:
silence is prayer,
prayer is faith,
faith is love,
love is service,
the fruit of service is peace.
—Mother Teresa

The best way to find yourself is to lose yourself in the
service of others.
—Mahatma Gandhi

In Japan, broken objects are often repaired with gold.
The flaw is seen as a unique piece of the object's history,
which adds to its beauty. Consider this when you feel
broken.
—Author unknown

Wabi-Sabi and *Kintsugi*

When I was researching for my TEDx Talk about the illusion of perfection, I came across a Japanese concept called *wabi-sabi*. Japanese culture places a high value on aesthetics, and Japanese notions of what makes an object beautiful differ from those of the West. The practice of *wabi-sabi* is deeply ingrained in Japanese culture and hard to describe, but the best approximation is "the appreciation of things that are imperfect." Just like in nature, life is imperfect, inconsistent, and impermanent. In our Western mindset, we tend to see these things as wrong or bad. We think our lives should be predictable and consistent and that things should go as planned. But *wabi-sabi* asks us to uphold imperfection as something beautiful in its own right.

I remember feeling so moved by this idea. It aligned wonderfully with my TEDx Talk and what I had come to learn throughout my life: that there is no such thing as perfect.

As I dug deeper, I came across a form of Japanese art that reflects a similar ideology to *wabi-sabi*, called *kintsugi*. *Kintsugi* is the practice of repairing broken pottery with lacquer mixed with powdered gold. Like *wabi-sabi*, *kintsugi* does not discard something because it is imperfect or broken. Something new and even more beautiful, with shimmering veins, is made out of the pieces. The brokenness is not hidden, but illuminated. In that way, the shattered pieces are honored as part of the object's history.

What would it be like if we did this with our lives? If we chose to pick up the pieces after we were broken, and we made something beautiful? If we displayed our repaired cracks for the world to see, knowing it was not a sign of weakness, but of strength and growth?

For the little girl in me who stood on her front porch in the dark at age ten, watching her dad being taken away in an ambulance, this concept was revolutionary. At that moment, that girl did not know how to process what was happening or why; she just felt herself shatter into a thousand little pieces. But that was not the end of her story.

In this book, you have read a lot about the times in my life when I have felt broken. When my dad tried to take his life, my unhealthy relationship with a married man, my dysfunctional family, and the pleasing behaviors I developed to survive. Some of the fractures were bigger than others, but over the years, they compounded. It took me a long time to figure out how to pick up the broken pieces. Early on, I wanted to throw them away, to reject these aspects of my life that were hard to look at by sweeping them into the dustpan and tossing them in the garbage. When I finally read about *wabi-sabi*, I felt like I could finally understand myself.

With this realization, I wrote a poem, part of which I'd love to share with you.

> *Wabi-Sabi is the Japanese art*
> *Where perfection is seen in every part*
> *Broken pieces on the floor*
> *No longer unseen or ignored*
>
> *Pieces handled with loving care*
> *Worked with in ways that others have not dared*
> *Seen as precious, valuable, and real*
> *This art and philosophy are the total deal*
>
> *Perfection perceived in people's lives seemed broken*
> *Experiences that have not been spoken*
> *A wound not damaged?*
> *A crack*
> *Not a flaw?*
> *These things so raw?*

Today I tell you the story of all that is true
I believe for me and for you
You are here and so am I to make a beautiful life
We can handle life's struggles and strife.

Just because something in my life was hard—or felt broken—did not mean I was worthless or that my life should be trashed. Instead, I was being presented with opportunities to create something even more beautiful, to find wholeness by repairing the pieces with shimmering gold. To see sacredness in my complications and imperfections. I think *wabi-sabi* and *kintsugi* are the most beautiful analogies for how we can relate to our human experience.

Turning to the God of Second Chances is the same as gently gathering our pieces and inlaying them with gold; it is about meeting those places that are deeply wounded and finding the blessings, the beauty, and the resources within all of them, knowing they are actually what make us whole.

What to Do with Your Brokenness

We all have broken pieces: trauma, moments that shatter us, and experiences that leave us overwhelmed, not knowing what to do or how to go on. You have read about a lot of these moments in the TEDx features. Whether they are fractures caused by the world, our family, or ourselves, our cracks accumulate over time. And if we do not find some way to transform the brokenness, it can weigh us down. So how do we pick ourselves up and heal with gold? Looking back at my life, I can identify one consistent theme that has helped me mend my brokenness: serving others.

Service is a big part of my life. When the voice spoke to me at the park about my purpose on this Earth, it said I was here to love, serve, and remember, like the song's lyrics. I believe that by serving from my wounded places, I find ways to integrate my pain and transform it.

I became aware of service when I was young and in need of help. A number of people generously reached out their hand and helped me when I could not help myself or did not know how. While I was growing up, my neighbors stepped in when my parents were unable to take care of me; my minister, Mary, took me under her wing and helped me cultivate the qualities of a mature woman; Judy Moore, my first therapist in Kansas City, was remarkable in helping me realize that I was more than the place I came from; my Sage Moms supported me through many life transitions. So many people have served me. In turn, I continue to serve others, and I feel myself heal and grow in the process.

That is why I think service is one of the best ways to repair ourselves with gold.

Serve through Your Woundedness

I have never sat down and asked myself, "What kind of service should I do now?" There has not been a plan. Instead, I have simply paid attention to my life and listened to what I felt called to do. Often, in hindsight, I can see how each service opportunity helped me work through something difficult I was facing at that time.

When I was older and working through my father's attempted suicide, I served on the board of directors for the Carson J. Spencer Foundation, a not-for-profit focused on men's mental health, well-being, and suicide prevention and awareness. In doing so, I came to terms with the pain I experienced as a young girl, and I hope I contributed meaningfully to an organization that prevents fathers from leaving their children behind.

When I was thirty-six years old, I wanted to become a mother. Due to my age, I was not sure if I would be able to get pregnant. At that time, I volunteered for a not-for-profit group that worked with new mothers, going to their homes with literature and resources, helping them manage this big life transition. By serving them, I started to feel that motherhood was possible for me. After miscarrying our first child, I had my son. When he was young, I struggled with feeling like I was not a good enough mother, so I joined his school's board of directors and other parent committees, bringing in speakers to support issues that were important to me. I was curious about asynchronous development and twice-exceptional kids and how to raise kind children who engaged in community service. I also took an interest in parenting skills for conflict resolution through the Love and Logic methodology. By helping myself adjust to some of the challenges of parenthood, I also served other parents who were asking the same questions.

When I left my job in sales and marketing to become a social worker, I was working through the chaos of my childhood, reaching for a deeper version of myself that was not defined by my life experiences. At that time, I worked with an amazing group of women. Their income was low, and many were on the welfare of the day, which was called TANF (Temporary Aid to Needy Families). Often, they faced a number of personal challenges, like being a single mom, living in a car, or struggling with mental illness or addiction. Every day I met with these women, I came home having learned so much. I was constantly challenged to think about life differently, and together we explored how they could continue getting up every day and meeting the world, working toward something more stable or fulfilling. Serving in that way was one of the most meaningful experiences of my life. It was not easy, but there was not a day when I did not receive more than I gave.

After social work, I became an independent coach, working primarily with women struggling with their identity, self-esteem, feelings of worthiness, traumatic experiences, and health challenges. With each client, I learned more about myself and grew in my own awareness around those issues. I often tell my clients that I am only a hair on my butt ahead of them. I am not special or different; I am merely diligent about my work, and I often encounter something one week—whether from a book or a thought leader—that then helps me support them the next week in whatever they are facing. It is like Spirit is right beside me, helping me stay just one step ahead in order to be of service but no further, lest I get ideas that I am "special" in any way. I am not. I am human, just like you, and I show up each day with humility in my heart, ready for the next lesson so that I can offer it back to someone who needs it.

Serving is my way of offering myself back to the world, but it is also my way of receiving. By serving others, I am given an opportunity to contribute what I am learning or have learned in my life. It is even more fulfilling to know that service has become an important value in my family. My husband is also dedicated to service, as is my son, who is currently serving as his fraternity's philanthropy chair.

Finding Your Service

There is a parable known as the allegory of the long spoon. Attributed to Rabbi Haim of Romshishok and others, the parable describes the difference between Heaven and Hell by putting people in the same scenario and revealing how they behave.[1] In the story, a group of people sit at a dining room table with a beautiful feast laid out before them. But when they go to eat, they realize their spoons are far too long to maneuver into their own mouths. Those in Hell starve. Those in Heaven learn that though the spoons are too long for their own mouths, they are perfectly sized to feed their neighbors across the way. By scooping the food on the plate across from them, then lifting a bite to that person's mouth, they feed one another and, in turn, are fed.

This is a story of generosity and service, of the nourishment we get by feeding one another and allowing ourselves to be fed. The desire to offer each other food comes from our own sense of hunger, just as my service comes from my brokenness and provides others with a path toward *kintsugi*.

So, what do you do with your shattering moments? The times when life brought you to your knees, when you questioned whether or not you could go on? The experiences that are scarred on your soul and might feel frightening to reveal to others, yet they leave you hungry for something more?

Finding your own kind of service is a creative practice. Only you can know how your brokenness can be offered back to the world through something wholesome. My own examples of service have often taken the form of my vocation, but that might not be the case for you. You might be involved in an organization on the side that uplifts some area of your life, as I did with Charlie's school board. Or maybe you offer your service through one of the oldest, most precious customs: sharing your story.

When I started participating in the TEDx world six years ago, I had no idea what I was getting myself into. I never knew I would become a co-curator for an event; I never knew I would share my own story; I never knew I would usher hundreds of others into using their voices to share ideas and stories. Sometimes, there is nothing more powerful than hearing someone share their story and seeing yourself reflected in it. You realize you are not alone and that there is a way forward in this crazy experience called life. Although I did not know it right away, I wanted to use my own voice in a way that was productive and supportive, as I did on that stage and am doing in this book. And I wanted to encourage other women to use their voices. I wanted to show up in the service of stories.

Stories as Service

When I think of all the TEDx speakers I have encountered over the years, a feeling of joy washes over me. I feel so much gratitude for the things I have learned that I previously did not know anything about, like the unbelievably tragic Tulsa massacre, climate change (did you know it takes ninety gallons of water to make one steak?), human trafficking, and neuroscience. Even more than the educational components, I have learned so much from our speakers about human potential, spirit, and resilience. It fills me up to watch women take that stage with the knowledge that they have something meaningful to contribute. If there is one thing I have learned from co-curating TEDx Talks for six years, it is that there is nothing more powerful than a woman standing on stage, sharing her ideas and spreading them for the world to hear.

I also get joy from seeing ripples of service unfolding in the world. Like the Bible says in Luke 6:38, "Give, and it shall be given unto you: good measure, pressed down and shaken together and running over, shall men give into your bosom. For with the same measure that ye mete, therewith it shall be measured to you again."[2] When we show up and serve from a place of humility, without the expectation of getting anything in return, we can offer what is needed at any moment. And those good deeds come back to us in the form of our own nourishment.

Service is about giving yourself, or something you possess, to another. Whether that is your time, your talent, or your treasures, consider the ways in which you can serve, and let go of expectations regarding how it will go. I promise that when you come to the world in this way, you will feel those broken pieces inside of you start to stitch back together, glistening and golden. It is not always easy. There are bumps in the road, and the journey is not perfect. But it is worth it, every time. You will never lose by serving, and when you are there for others, the bounty will come back to you tenfold.

Whatever service means to you, let it be a guiding light for healing your own woundedness.

TEDx Feature: Sally Spencer-Thomas, "Stopping Suicide with Story"

Sally Spencer-Thomas is a remarkable woman. I had the pleasure of meeting her in an interview for the board of directors for her not-for-profit organization, the Carson J. Spencer Foundation, which works to support men's mental health and suicide awareness and prevention. I liked her from the moment we met. We worked tirelessly to help men, youth, and organizations by spreading suicide prevention and awareness information. Sally, who used her brother's death by suicide as a springboard to make a difference, embodies *wabi-sabi*. She took her broken pieces and made something beautiful, something meaningful. Today, Sally is an international expert in her field, and we were privileged to have her on the TEDx stage in 2017.

At the start of Sally's talk, the stage was dark. She asked everyone to imagine being alone—all alone—in a dark, cold room. "The air is stagnant and smells foul. The only sound you can hear are the voices echoing in your head. And that bitter taste in your mouth tastes like scorched coffee. There are no doors, there are no windows; there is no way out."

"This is what it often feels like," she said as the light started to illuminate her, from a pinprick to a wider circle, "when people are in the throes of depression or suicidal despair."

Sally's story grew more personal. On December 7th, while on maternity leave, she was preparing to go to a party with her students at Regis University. She was feeling excited, with a ham in tow that made the car smell like cloves, wearing an eighties Christmas sweater and gingerbread earrings, when her mother called. It was one of those calls no one wants to receive.

"Sally," her mom said, "pull over." Although it was a matter of moments, it felt like an eternity as Sally eased the car to the side of the road. After telling her mom that she could not wait any longer to hear the news, her mom said, "Our worst fears have been confirmed. Your brother has died of suicide."

Immediately, memories and emotions flooded in. *No, not Carson*, she thought over and over. He was her only sibling and her first memory, born on Christmas Eve, like a present to her. They had danced at her wedding to Whitney Houston's "I Will Always Love You."

Only four days before, Sally and her brother had sat down for a conversation. She and her family had read *The Unquiet Mind* by Kay Redfield Jamison, a story of the author's experience with bipolar. Telling Carson about the book, Sally had said they would find their way forward together, that there were people who had bipolar and lived successful lives. He had turned to her and responded, "But Sally, it is madness." Four days later, he was gone.

Although she did not know exactly what the comment meant, Sally knew her brother. He was persistent and determined. She knew that he would have persisted in finding something to help him through the long, dark night of the soul and continue fighting

246 | *Oh God of Second Chances*

against his bipolar condition. She did not believe he had lost hope that he could get well again; she believed that he had lost hope that he could get his *life* back again. That he feared that his business partners would not trust him anymore, that his friends would look at him funny.

When she considered this hopelessness, she felt angry that people who are fighting for their lives also have to deal with prejudice and misinformation about mental health from the public.

Years later, Sally had an experience that made her wonder what her brother's mental and emotional experience had really been like. A storm descended on her life, and her own mental health was circling the toilet bowl—she could not eat, or sleep, or taste food, or hear birds chirp. Her anxiety was overwhelming. All she could think to do was work harder. As a psychologist, she said she should have known better. She knew facts and theory and treatment, but in the darkest parts of her own depression, she did not know how to climb out of it.

Finally, her father reached out and recommended she take her own advice—get some help. She showed up at her national conference, where she had all these professional roles to play. Fortunately, her colleagues told her that she did not need to do it all. She mattered, just as she was. With their support, she found her way through.

Sally knows her family is not alone in this kind of journey—close to 50,000 people die of suicide each year. About a fifth of those people are veterans, and suicide is the second leading cause of death for youth and young adults ages ten to thirty-nine.

For every person who dies of suicide, there are, on average, 115 people exposed to that suicide, and twenty-five of them will have major life disruptions after that death: divorce, losing a job, getting kicked out of school, financial ruin. For every suicide death, there are twenty-five people who live through their attempts. Through these facts, Sally honed in on a critical piece related to the suicide attempt survivors. "They hold the answers of what it feels like to experience that level of suicidal despair, and more importantly, how to get through it. Many of these people go on to live full lives . . . and often it is the suicide crisis that is the turning point to help them get back into life."

But the problem, Sally pointed out, is that most families keep these stories in the closet because they feel ashamed, angry, or guilty about what happened. And because we do not share our stories, we fail to really see that something is deeply wrong in our society.

Sally believed that suicide prevention and the promotion of mental health promotion are among the most significant cross-cultural, multigenerational social justice issues of our times, and they often go unaddressed. By "social justice," she meant fundamental human rights—the right to have a job, to have homes and relationships, and to be a parent. She also included the right to practice responsibility in the community to support the common good.

Sally dove into some of the details of what social justice looks like for mental health. Our society, she explained, is drawn to quick fixes. To popping pills, forced treatment, short hospital stays, and interventions that often feel more like punishment than help. "Instead," she asked, "what if we saw people instead of diagnoses? What if we met people with compassion during their worst days? What if we put more research into the so-called 'alternative therapies?'"

She knew we could do better, and at the center of change were stories. Every important social movement included stories about people, their own experiences of life, and how change was possible. Stories help us make meaning, help us have ownership and empowerment over the confusing or chaotic things that happen to us. And when we share our stories in community, we gather people around us and make them feel seen and connected.

Stories are how we can inlay our brokenness with gold.

Through this fundamental shift in culture via storytelling, Sally said, we can shift the culture from bias and discrimination to dignity and empowerment, one story at a time.

Sally then extended an invitation. Acknowledging that we are all touched by this conversation in some form or fashion, she invited everyone to join her on a social justice journey. Using PowerPoint images projected behind her, she shared examples of people who were her personal heroes because they told their stories to inspire change. They included the individual who survived a suicide attempt and went on to write books, a photographer who also survived an attempt and captured portraits of other survivors, and an award-winning documentary filmmaker who suffered two losses and focused on portraying new narratives about bipolar and suicide.

In closing, Sally invited the people in the theater to participate in an exercise. Everyone took out their phones, and after the lights were dimmed, Sally asked those who had lost a loved one to suicide to hold up their illuminated phones, shining their light in the darkness. She told them that their stories and loved ones mattered. Then, she invited people who had walked the long, dark night of the soul to raise their phones—those with experiences of mental illness, depression, eating disorders, overwhelming stress and anxiety, OCD. Their lights represented hope and the ability to support others who were struggling. Finally, she encouraged those who supported mental illness and suicide prevention to hold up their light as a symbol of being there for someone struggling in the dark.

As a call to action, Sally asked everyone to be a beacon and draw others to this cause. To hold their light or hold someone else's until they were strong enough to take up the charge once more. "Be the light," she said with that courageous heart of hers, "or bring the light, because light is life."

Light is life, and Sally is someone wholly dedicated to service and the preservation of human life. Her brokenness became her greatest beauty, and it radiates out into the community, inspiring an important shift that our world desperately needs.

How can your brokenness become its own beacon for good?

The Practice: Love, Serve, Remember (Part Two)

Okay, if you are paying attention, you might realize that Chapter Four's practice was *also* called Love, Serve, Remember. That is the great thing about these three intentions—there are always more ways to practice!

Here are three more suggestions for how you can continue to open the gifts of love, service, and remembrance in your life. In doing so, pay particular attention to how your own wounds start to soften and maybe even knit themselves back together with gold.

1. Meditation—A loving-kindness meditation is one of the most powerful ways to open your heart to love from yourself and others. Reading this meditation on a regular basis will expand your awareness and the remembrance of who you truly are and build compassion for others as well [3].
2. Random acts of kindness—In her TEDx Talk "Nourishment of the Soul," our very own Brook Jones shared how random acts of kindness (RAC) helped her shift from a place of darkness and fear and transform her life. I highly recommend watching

her talk [4] and also visiting the RAC website for creative ideas for spreading kindness [5].

3. Volunteer to heal your broken pieces—Finding a way to serve from our seeming woundedness changes how we see ourselves in relation to our circumstances. If you are struggling in any area of your life, ask yourself who else might be struggling in the same or a similar situation. Explore opportunities to give your time, talents, or treasures to others.

    a. Volunteer your time
    b. Share something you are good at with other individuals
    c. Donate clothes, money, or resources to a local charity

Remember—I am whole, perfect, and complete; God don't make no junk!

Oh God of Second Chances, may I serve—not to receive, but to give of my wounds and my heart.

11

Thank God of Second Chances for (Infinite) Second Chances

Somewhere over the rainbow way up high
There is a land that I heard of once in a lullaby.
Somewhere over the rainbow skies are blue
And the dreams that you dare to dream really do come true.

Someday I'll wish upon a star
And wake up where the clouds are far behind me.
Where troubles melt like lemon drops
Away above the chimney tops
That is where you will find me.

Somewhere over the rainbow bluebirds fly
Birds fly over the rainbow
Why then, oh, why can't I?

If happy little bluebirds fly
Beyond the rainbow
Why, oh, why can't I?
- Judy Garland, "Somewhere Over the Rainbow"

I love the title of this book—*Oh God of Second Chances, Here I Am Again*. Every day when I finish journaling, I think of that phrase: *Here I am again, for the 25,000th time.*

Whether it is fresh feelings of self-doubt, negative thoughts, stuff I did or did not do that day, being a bad mom or a bitchy wife, not living up to expectations, taking things personally, judging others or myself . . . I am constantly asking for another chance. I am constantly forgetting who I am, what this is all about, and how to be present to the blessing of my life. Like I said, I am a hair on my hiney ahead of some people, but that is it. I have a lot of work to do, too. Just because I teach and coach does not mean I am without challenges.

My hope for this book is that you take away something that became clear to me when I was writing it: none of us are alone. Whether my stories resonated with you, or one of the TEDx features, we are all messy humans struggling to get by. The details of our stories might be different, but the general themes are the same. We all want to be whole, happy, and healthy, and we frequently stumble through life trying to find our way. When you hear your story in someone else's, it changes everything. There is no greater healing than knowing you are not alone in whatever you are facing.

I have done my best to be honest, vulnerable, and authentic. I have talked about a lot of different times when I have fallen down—an affair, drug and alcohol use, all the things that have led me to the person I am now. Along my journey, there is one recurring theme: I have been blessed with second chances, third chances, five-thousandth chances. I have always known that I have a choice about whether or not I want another chance, just as you do. Some people believe that you are supposed to have life figured out after getting knocked on your ass the first time, but that has not been not my experience or my clients'. We often need to return to the same lessons again and again before things start to change. The real question is this: are you willing to get back up again and take the next chance?

What to Do with Your Second Chances

Being given a second chance is a generous gift from the Universe. Not every second chance will mean a great transformation in our lives, but sometimes, when everything aligns just right, we do incredible things with our second chances.

Let us have a quick look back at our inspiring TEDx features and what these women did with their second chances.

In Chapter One, which was about courage, Pat Jacques decided to stop assuming everything about her was inherently wrong and instead declare everything as inherently *right*.

In Chapter Two, which was about leading with the heart, Phoenix Jackson listened deeply to her heart and found herself on an incredible journey of dance, spirit, and inspiration.

In Chapter Three, which was about vulnerability, Nikki Dority explored what self-care really looks like with a bipolar condition and in our manic culture.

In Chapter Four, which was on remembering, Dafna Michaelson Jenet remembered the importance of service in our communities, and Maggie Johnson remembered her future through poetry and hope.

In Chapter Five, which was on the illusion of perfection, Mary Jelkovsky burst the body image illusion of perfection and enjoyed a cup of mocha.

In Chapter Six, which was on surrender, Laura Thomas learned to surrender to her grief through theater, inviting audiences to join her in the process.

In Chapter Seven, which was on coming home to yourself, Betsy Wiersma explored the importance of our chosen families and how to build strong, lasting relationships.

In Chapter Eight, which was on the divine feminine, Haley Skiko demonstrated that the divine feminine means tapping into our vulnerabilities and knowing that is where our greatest strengths lie.

In Chapter Nine, which was on being a woman in today's world, Gretchen Gagel invited us into a new, supportive conversation around the treatment of working moms in our society.

In Chapter Ten, which was on service, Sally Spencer-Thomas shared how she turned her heartbreak into purpose by using stories to prevent suicide.

There are many unique, creative ways you can use your second chances in the world. Whether you follow a path that might lead you to a TEDx stage or your transformation remains quiet and personal, it all matters. Our choices matter, and we will never know the ripples we send out into the world by choosing to live fully. It is not just for your benefit. It is for everyone.

It All Comes Back to Courage

I started this book with courage, and there is a reason for that. It takes great courage to be in the world with an open heart, to be vulnerable, to be sensitive. Every day, I try to remember who I am and what I am meant to be and do on this planet. When I forget, I get back on the bike and remember. I remember that I come from something greater than this human experience; I remember that

Earth School can be consuming, but it is not who I am underneath it all.

Over the years, I have learned to quell my ego, who I thought I should be, and how I thought my life should go. From that surrender, I was able to see that my true home was not my family of origin, but a place inside of me that was always available, always ready to welcome me back. And in that home, I have both masculine and feminine parts that, when expressed in their divinity, help me feel whole and complete as an empowered human. There is nothing inside of me that is either/or—I am *all* the pieces of me, and they each deserve to be honored and respected.

And though it is fucking tough being a woman in today's world, I remember that the toughness of women is what our world needs right now. From our menstrual cycles to our challenging history in the world to the experience of childbirth, we are capable of so much, and though there are still inequities and hardships, we have come a long way over the last fifty years. We are so much more than our roles and labels, including the labels we place on ourselves to describe our woundedness. When we are able to transform our woundedness by serving others, we make a difference in the world, and our lives start to glimmer with gold.

Through all of these lessons, I am so grateful that I have always trusted there was something more to me, something guiding me that I could trust every single day, something that would extend a hand to me and pull my ass off the floor so that I could keep going. Whether it is God's grace or Spirit, it really does not make a difference. *That* is the greatest gift in my life—knowing there is a Source that loves me, guides me, and protects me. And it is there for you, too. With its infinite second chances, there is something that will help you stand, wipe your tears, and ask you to try again. Because you deserve to feel like a meaningful part of this world.

As I sit here, heart full and eyes moist, one last message comes to mind. A final prayer, brimming with gratitude:

Oh God of Second Chances . . . thank you for second chances.

Wishing you a full life, dear reader, where your beauty shines for the benefit of the entire world.

Acknowledgments

This work is dedicated to the family that I chose at birth—Dad, Mom, and Mike. Without you and all of us and our shit, good, bad, and ugly, I could not be me and wouldn't be doing what I do in this world. Thank you for your love, the laughs, and the many lessons. I love you.

I am so grateful for the love and support of my many teachers, therapists, and mentors. Dr. Judy Moore and Mary Omwake, thank you for seeing me and helping me see the potential in myself and in my life. Your unconditional love and support changed everything. Dr. Jean East, Susan Kenney, Aspen Decew, the leadership team at the Leadership Circle, Cathy Hawk, Deb Haynie—for your teachings and mentorship, I am forever grateful.

To my Sage Moms—Betty, Karon, Nancy, Dixie, Rozy, Bonnie and Carol Jean, Martha—how blessed I feel to have had your unconditional love and support all these years. One day, I will write the book of all of our crazy times together and the many lessons and blessings that we have enjoyed together. I love you!

Notes

Introduction: The Power of New Beginnings

Natasha Bedingfield, "Unwritten," *Unwritten* (Phonogenic, 2004).
[1] Frank L. Baum, *The Wonderful Wizard of Oz* (George M. Hill Company, 1900).

Chapter One: A Little Courage, Please

Frank L. Baum, *The Wonderful Wizard of Oz* (George M. Hill Company, 1900), quoted on *Goodreads*, accessed November 20, 2019,www.goodreads.com/quotes/31120-you-have-plenty-of-courage-i-am-sure-answered-oz.
[1] *Merriam-Webster*, s.v. "courage," accessed November 20, 2019.
[2] Luke 12:32 (21st Century King James Version; all subsequent citations are from this version).
[3] Matthew 7:7.
[4] Daniel Pink, *A Whole New Mind: Why Right-Brainers Will Rule the Future* (Riverhead Books, 2006).
[5] Brené Brown, *I Thought It Was Just Me (But It Isn't): Making the*

Journey from "What Will People Think?" to "I Am Enough" (Avery, 2007).

[6] Reeti Banerjee, "54 Courage Quotes That Will Motivate You." *EliteColumn*, accessed November 20, 2019, www.elitecolumn. com/courage-quotes/.

[7] Deborah Adele, *The Yamas & Niyamas: Exploring Yoga's Ethical Practice* (On-Word Bound Books, 2009).

[8] *We Bought a Zoo*, directed by Cameron Crowe, performances by Matt Damon and Scarlett Johansson (20th Century Fox, 2011).

[9] Jill Bolte Taylor, *My Stroke of Insight: A Brain Scientist's Personal Journey* (Penguin Books, 2009).

[1o] Jill Bolte Taylor, *Whole Brain Living: The Anatomy of Choice and the Four Characters That Drive Our Lives* (Hay House, Inc., 2021).

[11] Marianne Williamson, *A Return to Love: Reflections on the Principles of "A Course in Miracles"* (HarperOne, reissue ed., 1996).

[12] Erin McCarthy, "Roosevelt's 'The Man in the Arena.'" *Mental Floss*, accessed December 3, 2021, www.mentalfloss.com/article/63389/roosevelts-man-arena.

[13] Brené Brown, *Daring Greatly: How the Courage to Be Vulnerable Transforms the Way We Live, Love, Parent, and Lead* (Avery, 2015).

[14] "Eleanor Roosevelt Quotes," *Goodreads*, accessed January 4, 2022, www.goodreads.com/quotes/3823-you-gain-strength-courage-and-confidence-by-every-experience-in.

[15] Pat Jacques, "What If Everything About You Is Inherently Right?" *Youtube*, uploaded by TEDx Talks, January 5, 2019, https://www.youtube.com/watch?v=qtH8HNADMEg&t=1s.

Chapter Two: Leading with the Heart

"L. Frank Baum Quotes." *Goodreads*, accessed January 4, 2022, www.goodreads.com/quotes/220560-i-shall-take-the-heart-for-brains-do-not.

[1] Rick Hanson, "Confronting the Negativity Bias," *Rick Hanson, PhD*, accessed January 4, 2022, www.rickhanson.net/how-your-brain-makes-you-easily-intimidated/.

www.psychologytoday.com/us/articles/200306/
our-brains-negative-bias.

[2] Don Miguel Ruiz, *The Four Agreements: A Practical Guide to Personal Freedom (A Toltec Wisdom Book)* (Amber-Allen Publishing, 2001).

[3] Jack Kornfield, "Your Mind: Friend or Foe?" *Jack Kornfield,* accessed January 4, 2022, www.jackkornfield.com/your-mind-friend-or-foe/.

[4] *Merriam-Webster.* s.v. "intuition," accessed January 4, 2022.

[5] "5 Ways to Develop Your Intuition," *Deepak Chopra,* accessed January 4, 2022, www.deepakchopra.com/articles/5-ways-to-develop-your-intuition/.

[6] "Coherence." *HeartMath Institute*, accessed January 4, 2022, www.heartmath.org/articles-of-the-heart/the-math-of-heartmath/coherence/.

[7] HeartMath Institute, "An Overview of Research Conducted by the HeartMath Institute." *Science of the Heart: Vol. 2 (1993-2016), Exploring the Role of the Heart in Human Performance*, accessed January 4, 2022, www.heartmath.org/resources/downloads/science-of-the-heart/.

[8] "The Science of HeartMath." *HeartMath*, accessed January 4, 2022, www.heartmath.com/science/.

Chapter Three: Come to the Edge

[1] "Guillaume Apollinaire Quotes," *Goodreads*, accessed January 5, 2022, www.goodreads.com/quotes/17760-come-to-the-edge-he-said-we-can-t-we-re-afraid.

[2] "Brené Brown: 'You Cannot Get to Courage Without Walking Through Vulnerability' (VIDEO)." *Huffpost*, accessed January 5, 2021, www.huffpost.com/entry/brene-brown-vulnerability_n_3909420.

[3] Brené Brown, *Daring Greatly: How the Courage to Be Vulnerable Transforms the Way We Live, Love, Parent, and Lead* (Avery, 2015).

[4] Brené Brown, *The Gifts of Imperfection: Let Go of Who You Think*

You Are Supposed to Be and Embrace Who You Are (Simon and Schuster, 2010).
[5] Brown, *Daring Greatly.*
[6] "The Drama Triangle: What is the Dreaded Drama Triangle (DDT)?" *TED**The Empowerment Dynamic*, accessed January 5, 2022, www.powerofted.com/drama-triangle/.

Chapter Four: Why Have We Come to Earth?
[1] John Astin. "Love, Serve, and Remember." *Remembrance* (CD Baby,1991).
[2] "How Hemi-Sync Works: Revealing Research for Peak Human Performance." *Hemi-Synch*, accessed January 5, 2022, www.hemi-sync.com/learn/how-hemi-sync-works/.
[3] Portia Nelson, *There's a Hole in My Sidewalk: The Romance of Self-Discovery* (Atria Books/Beyond Words Publishing, 1994).
[4] Leadership Circle, www.leadershipcircle.com/en/
[5] Thomas Gray, "Ode on a Distant Prospect of Eton College."(1768) *Poetry Foundation*, accessed January 5, 2022, www.poetryfoundation.org/poems/44301/ode-on-a-distant-prospect-of-eton-college.
[6] "Leadership Denver." *Leadership Denver*, accessed January 5, 2022, www.denverleadership.org/leadershipdenver/.
[7] Braden Gregg, *Fractal Time: The Secret of 2012 and a New World Age* (Hay House Inc., 2010).
[8] Luke 12:32.
[9] Robert Rosenthal, "Expectancy Effect by Experimenters," *Encyclopedia of Statistics in Behavioral Science* (2005). *Wiley Stats-Ref: Statistic Reference Online* (2014), accessed January 5, 2022, www.doi.org/10.1002/9781118445112.stat06726.
[1o] "Pygmalion Effect," *Wikipedia*, accessed January 5, 2022, www.en.wikipedia.org/wiki/Pygmalion_effect.
Chapter Five: The Illusion of Perfectionism
Leo Tolstoy, *Anna Karenina* (Penguin Classics, 2004), quoted

on *Goodreads*, accessed January 14, 2022, www.goodreads.com/work/quotes/2507928.

[1] Brené Brown, *The Gifts of Imperfection: Let Go of Who You Think You Are Supposed to Be and Embrace Who You Are* (Simon and Schuster, 2010).

[2] Brown, *The Gifts of Imperfection*.

[3] "Test How Self-Compassionate You Are." *Self-Compassion: Dr. Kristin Neff*, accessed January 5, 2022, www.self-compassion.org/self-compassion-test/.

[4] Rebecca Rosen, "Are You Carrying an Energetic Burden?" (unpublished manuscript, March 5, 2021).

[5] Tara Brach, *Radical Acceptance: Embracing Your Life with the Heart of a Buddha* (Random House Publishing Group, 2004).

[6] Amy Summerville, "Is Comparison Really the Thief of Joy? New Research Explores Why Comparison Gets Us Down and How to Voice This." *Psychology Today*, March 21, 2019, accessed January 5, 2022, www.psychologytoday.com/us/blog/multiple-choice/201903/is-comparison-really-the-thief-joy.

[7] Kristin Neff, "The Space Between Self-Esteem and Self Compassion." *YouTube*, uploaded by TEDx Talks, February 6, 2013, www.youtube.com/watch?v=IvtZBUSplr4.

[8] Kristin Neff, https://self-compassion.org/category/exercises/#exercis

[9] "Exercise 2: Self-Compassion Break." *Self-Compassion: Dr. Kristin Neff*, accessed January 13, 2022, www.self-compassion.org/exercise-2-self-compassion-break/.

Chapter Six: The Surrender

"Marianne Williamson Quotes," *Goodreads*, accessed January 5, 2022, www.goodreads.com/quotes/387102-something-amazing-happens-when-we-surrender-and-just-love-we.

Garth Brooks. "The River." *Ropin' the Wind* (Nashville: Capitol Records Nashville, 1991).

[1] Nicole Nordeman. "River God." *Nicole Nordeman: The Ultimate Collection* (Sparrow Records, 2009).

[2] "No 'God Spot' in Brain, Spirituality Linked to Right Parietal Lobe," *Huffpost*, April 20, 2012, accessed January 5, 2022, www.huffpost.com/entry/god-spot-in-brain-is-not-_n_1440518.

[3] Andrew Newberg, *How God Changes Your Brain: Breakthrough Findings from a Leading Neuroscientist* (Ballantine Books, 2010).

[4] Helen Schucman, *A Course in Miracles* (also referred to as ACIM or the Course) (Course in Miracles Society, 1976).

[5] Hiren Chauhan, "Broken Dreams by Lauretta P. Burns." *Thoughts & Feelings*, October 4, 2011, accessed January 5, 2022, www.chauhanhiren.blogspot.com/2011/10/broken-dreams-by-lauretta-p-burns.html.

[6] "Rumi Quotes." *Goodreads*, accessed January 11, 2022, www.goodreads.com/quotes/1299504-i-said-what-about-my-eyes-he-said-keep-them.

[7] "A Reason, Season, or Lifetime Friendship Poem," accessed January 11, 2022, https://bereaveddadsnetwork.com/books-resources/f/Ca-reason-a-season-a-lifetime-by-brian-drew-chalker.

[8] "Serenity Prayer, Attributed to Reinhold Neibuhr." *Prayer Foundation*, accessed January 11, 2022, www.prayerfoundation.org/dailyoffice/serenity_prayer_full_version.htm/.

[9] Emma Wall, "A River Meditation for Letting Go," *Ocean Flow Fitness*, August 27, 2017, accessed January 17, 2022, www.oceanflowfitness.com/blog/flow/meditation-mindfulness/a-river-meditation-for-letting-go/.

Chapter Seven: Three Clicks of the Ruby Red Cowboy Boots—Coming Home to Yourself

The Wizard of Oz. Directed by Victor Fleming, performance by Judy Garland (Metro-Goldwyn-Mayer, 1939).

[1] Maria Connolly, "Old Hindu Legend, Author Unknown." *Neways Somatic Psychotherapy & Coaching*, accessed January 5,

2022, www.newayscenter.com/wp-content/uploads/2021/05/
OLD-HINDU-LEGEND.pdf.
[2] Leon F. Seltzer, "The Path to Unconditional Self-Ac-
ceptance: How Do You Fully Accept Yourself When
You Do Not Know How?" *Psychology Today*, September 10, 2008, accessed January 5, 2022, www.psy-
chologytoday.com/us/blog/evolution-the-self/200809/
the-path-unconditional-self-acceptance.
[3] Glennon Doyle, *Untamed* (The Dial Press, 2020), quoted on
Goodreads, accessed January 5, 2022, www.goodreads.com/
author/quotes/17099759.Glennon_Doyle.

Chapter Eight: The Divine Feminine
Lucy Pearce, *Burning Woman* (Womancraft Publishing, 2016),
quoted on *Goodreads*, accessed January 5, 2022, www.goodreads.
com/work/quotes/50512920-burning-woman.
[1] John A. Sanford, *The Invisible Partner: How the Male and Female
in Each of Us Affects Our Relationships* (Paulist Press, 1979).
[2] Nathaniel Branden, *If You Could Hear What I Cannot Say:
Learning to Communicate with the Ones You Love* (Bantam, 1983).
[3] Patricia Evans, *The Verbally Abusive Relationship: How to Recognize It and How to Respond* (Adams Media, 1992).
[4] Evans, *The Verbally Abusive Relationship*.
[5] Christiane Northrup, *Dodging Energy Vampires: An Empath's
Guide to Evading Relationships that Drain You and Restoring Your
Health and Power* (Hay House Inc., 2019).
[6] Christiane Northrup, "An Empath's Best Protec-
tion Against Energy Vampires: 10 Strategies for Protecting Yourself," *Christiane Northrup, M.D.*, March 5,
2019, accessed January 5, 2022, www.drnorthrup.com/
an-empaths-best-protection-against-energy-vampires/.
[7] Lena Schmidt, "How to Find the Balance Between Your
Masculine & Feminine Energy," *Deepak Chopra*, May 31,
2019, accessed January 5, 2022, www.chopra.com/articles/

how-to-find-the-balance-between-your-masculine-feminine-en-
ergy.

Chapter Nine: Being A Woman in Today's World
"Wild And Free Quotes," *Wild & Rise*, quoted on *Goodreads*,
accessed January 17, 2022, www.goodreads.com/quotes/tag/
wild-and-free.
Woolf, Virginia. *A Room of One's Own* (Penguin, 1945), quoted
on *Goodreads*, accessed January 5, 2022, www.goodreads.com/
work/quotes/1315615-a-room-of-one-s-own.
[1] "The Truth about Marriage." *Oprah*, May 9, 2006,
accessed January 13. 2022, www.oprah.com/oprahshow/
the-truth-about-marriage/all.
[2] "Bechdel Test." *Wikipedia*, accessed January 5, 2022, www.
en.wikipedia.org/wiki/Bechdel_test.
[3] Irene Levine, "Why Are Women So Mean to Each Other?
Some Mean Girls Never Grow Up," *Psychology Today*,
August 13, 2010, accessed January 5, 2022, www.psy-
chologytoday.com/us/blog/the-friendship-doctor/201008/
why-are-women-so-mean-each-other.
[4] Hara Estroff Marano, "Big Bad Bully: Bullies Aim to Inflict
Pain. But Eventually, the One Most Hurt by Bullying Is the
Bully Himself," *Psychology Today*, September 1, 1995, accessed
January 5, 2022, www.psychologytoday.com/intl/articles/199509/
big-bad-bully.

Chapter Ten: Healing Through Service
"Mother Teresa Quote," *PassItOn*, accessed January 5, 2022,
www.passiton.com/inspirational-quotes/7232-the-simple-path-
silence-is-prayer-prayer-is.
"Mahatma Gandhi Quotes," *Goodreads*, accessed
January 5, 2022, www.goodreads.com/
quotes/11416-the-best-way-to-find-yourself-is-to-lose-yourself.
Alex Hales, "In Japan Broken Objects Are Often

Repaired with Gold," *Mind Journal*, accessed January 5, 2022, www.themindsjournal.com/
in-japan-broken-objects-are-often-repaired-with-gold/.
[1] "Allegory of the Long Spoons." *Wikipedia*, accessed
January 5, 2022, https://en.wikipedia.org/wiki/
Allegory_of_the_long_spoons.
[2] Luke 6:38.
[3] https://palousemindfulness.com/docs/lovingkindness-med.pdf
[4] https://www.youtube.com/watch?v=NDfH9sA1lB8
[5] https://www.randomactsofkindness.org/kindness-ideas.

Chapter Eleven: Thank God of Second Changes for (Infinite) Second Chances
Judy Garland. "Somewhere Over the Rainbow," Written by Harold Arlen and E.Y. Harburg, *The Wizard of Oz* (Leo Feist, Inc., 1939).

Featured and Recommended TEDx Talks

Featured in the Book:

Chapter One: Pat Jacques, "What If Everything About Me Is Inherently Right?" (2018)
https://www.ted.com/talks/
pat_jacques_what_if_everything_about_me_is_inherently_right

Chapter Two: Phoenix Jackson, "The Spirit of the Moment" (2016)
https://www.youtube.com/watch?v=v5vKNn_HVkc

Chapter Three: Nicole Dority, "The Destigmatization of Mania in a Manic Culture" (2020)
https://www.ted.com/talks/

nicole_dority_the_destigmatization_of_mania_in_a_manic_culture

Chapter Four: Dafna Michaelson Jenet, "50 in 52 Journey" (2010)
https://www.youtube.com/watch?v=ZMU75W8Bgs0

Chapter Four: Maggie Johnson, "Seventeen in Quarantine" (2020)
https://www.ted.com/talks/
maggie_johnson_seventeen_in_quarantine

Chapter Five: Mary Jelkovsky, "Our Bodies Are Not an Image" (2019)
https://www.ted.com/talks/
mary_jelkovsky_our_bodies_are_not_an_image

Chapter Six: Laura Thomas, "Navigating the World of Grief" (2019)
https://www.ted.com/talks/
laura_thomas_navigating_the_world_of_grief

Chapter Seven: Betsy Wiersma, "Choose Your Family, Change Your Life" (2019)
https://www.ted.com/talks/
betsy_wiersma_choose_your_family_change_your_life

Chapter Eight: Haley Skiko, "How Vulnerability Unleashes Freedom" (2021)
https://www.ted.com/talks/
haley_skiko_how_vulnerability_unleashes_freedom

Chapter Nine: Gretchen Gagel, "The Power to Change the Working Mom Conversation" (2016)

https://www.youtube.com/watch?v=12-plyTMBrs

Chapter Ten: Sally Spencer-Thomas, "Stopping Suicide with Story" (2017)
https://www.ted.com/talks/
sally_spencer_thomas_stopping_suicide_with_story

Recommended:

Brené Brown, "The Power of Vulnerability" (2010)
https://www.ted.com/talks/
brene_brown_the_power_of_vulnerability

Jean East, "Leading with Head, Heart and Soul" (2018)
https://www.youtube.com/watch?v=6xuXsKPHgmY

Brooke Jones, "Nourishment of the Soul" (2017) https://www.ted.com/talks/brooke_jones_nourishment_of_the_soul

Kristen Neff, "The Space Between Self-Esteem and Self Compassion" (2013) https://www.youtube.com/watch?v=IvtZBUSplr4

ABOUT THE AUTHOR

Christy Belz, MSW, is an empowerment coach and entrepreneur who is passionate about guiding people to live their best, most authentic selves personally, professionally and developmentally. Named one of Colorado's Top 25 Most Powerful Women in Business in 2020, she is also a TEDx Speaker and a co-curator of TEDxCherryCreek, through which she encourages women to share their voice. Founder of the transformational UPROOT course, she can often be found reading the latest book in the personal growth and leadership genres or walking her dog in nature while keeping an eye out for heart-shaped leaves. Christy lives in Denver with her husband and son.